D0987189

HOLINESS
AND
JUSTICE

An Interpretation of Plato's **Euthyphro**

Laszlo Versényi

UNIVERSITY
PRESS OF
AMERICA

LANHAM • NEW YORK • LONDON

Copyright © 1982 by

University Press of America,™ Inc.

4720 Boston Way
Lanham, MD 20706

3 Henrietta Street
London WC2E 8LU England

Library of Congress Cataloging in Publication Data

Versenyi, Laszlo.
  Holiness and justice.

  Bibliography: p.
    1. Plato. Euthyphro. 2. Piety–History. I. Title.
B370.V47   179'.9   81–43830
ISBN 0–8191–2316–1   AACR2
ISBN 0–8191–2317–X (pbk.)

CONTENTS

PREFACE

The Euthyphro has, in some respects, a rather special position among Plato's early dialogues. Its subject, the concept of
holiness or piety, is clearly of exceptional relevance to Plato's
defense of Socrates against the charges on which he was tried and
convicted. Yet not only does this dialogue fail, at least ostensibly, to provide a definition of this concept, but piety, unlike
the other virtues discussed in the companion dialogues of the
Euthyphro, never receives much attention let alone a clear definition elsewhere. In the Republic it is not even included in the
list of cardinal virtues Plato considers complete.

In view of the importance of this particular virtue for
Socrates' trial, Plato's failure to define it and his relative
neglect of the subject are at least puzzling. Did Socrates, or
Plato, consider piety a virtue, and if so why is it left undefined here and ignored in the Republic? Or did they consider it
no virtue at all, and if so why is such a conclusion never clearly stated and argued for in any of the dialogues?

Even the negative conclusions actually reached in the
Euthyphro present problems, in that some of the definitions that
are rejected as untenable here are used in the Apology in an attempt to show that Socrates was indeed pious in terms of such
definitions. How can such prima facie inconsistencies between
two dialogues written at about the same time be reconciled? Does
the Euthyphro contribute anything to Plato's defense of Socrates,
and if so does it strengthen or weaken the arguments used in the
Apology?

These are some of the questions that reading the Euthyphro
in its historical context raises. But there is an equally serious
unhistorical, or not merely historical, problem involved in study-
ing the Euthyphro today.

Unlike the other virtues extensively discussed in Plato's
early and middle dialogues—wisdom, courage, temperance and justice—which are still widely regarded to be virtues, piety's very
status as a necessary component of human excellence is rather
controversial in our secular age. In consequence, interpreters
cannot simply take for granted the contemporary reader's interest
in the subject of the Euthyphro but they have to justify their
preoccupation with this dialogue by showing that its study is of
great significance even to the modern reader who happens to be
uninterested in "historical" or merely "religious" questions in
the narrow senses of these words.

Fortunately, for all their superficial dissimilarity, these

problems of historical and contemporary relevance are so closely connected that an interpretation that solves the first will also resolve the second; at least that is what the following interpretation attempts to do. The definition of piety which I find implicit in the Euthyphro and seek to make explicit in this study explains, I believe, Plato's failure to offer a positive definition of piety anywhere in his dialogues and his omission of piety from the list of cardinal virtues in the Republic. At the same time it not only shows piety to be a universal, in its essence historically unconditioned virtue, but reveals the encounter between Euthyphro and Socrates as one that each age has to relive in its own way lest it run the danger of obscuring the very meaning of human excellence.

If successful, such a solution to the Euthyphro's problems should go some way toward reinstating this dialogue among the best of Plato's production. For at present, largely because of these unsolved problems, there is little consensus among readers as to the overall worth of the Euthyphro. Some regard it altogether worthless, a philosophical as well as artistic failure; others view it as a preparatory exercise for later revelations which are at best merely adumbrated here. There is no agreement among scholars even as to what the issues are for whose discussion the Euthyphro is supposed to lay the ground—ethical, religious, epistemological or metaphysical ones—and this uncertainty naturally affects all judgments concerning the dialogue's real message and worth.

In my view, the view this study presents and attempts to justify, the Euthyphro is a small but flawless work: It is one of Plato's most successful dialogues whose exquisitely harmonized form and content are altogether sufficient for resolving the issues it raises, and whose contribution to the discussion of ethical, religious, epistemological and even jurisprudential problems still ranks with the best the history of philosophy has to offer.

HISTORICAL BACKGROUND

We know that Socrates was tried and convicted on a charge of impiety, but what exactly impiety meant for the Greeks of his time is not easy to specify. Not because we do not have ample evidence to determine how the words asebes and anosios were used in fifth century Greece, but because the evidence tends to show that the traditional meaning of these terms which were crucial to Socrates' trial was so extended and, indeed, indefinitely extendable as to make piety just about incapable of being defined as a particular rather than all inclusive virtue.

The literal meaning of eusebeia (from eu: rightly, properly, well; and sebein: to fear, revere, be in awe of) is right reverence. He who reveres what is truly venerable, is in awe of what is truly awesome, abhors what is really awful and respects what is most worthy of respect, is eusebes. Etymologically eusebeia is an extremely flexible concept, almost a blanket term under which all virtuous behavior can be subsumed, and the actual use the Greeks made of this term fully exploited its literal potential. Although the gods and all that concerned them were certainly proper objects of eusebeia, and to this extent piety was a religious term even in the modern restricted sense of the word, eusebeia did not in fact necessarily involve a direct relationship of men to the gods or objects and acts directly pertaining to their worship in a narrow sense. It also required reverence toward the dead, the veneration of parents and ancestors, the proper relation toward all one's blood relatives, and indeed, in its most extended use, the right relationship of a man to all other members of his community. In its earliest appearance in Greek literature the term was defined with reference not to the gods but to justice, the virtue in which "the whole of virtue is brought together" (Theognis 145ff.), and at no time does later Greek usage provide us with narrow criteria that would allow us to distinguish between specifically "pious" actions and all other modes of behavior which might be considered virtuous without being necessarily pious at the same time.

And the same is true of hosiotes and its cognates. In Homer ou hosion means simply "not permitted".[1] Like ou themis the term conveys that something "is not done", i.e. is contrary to established custom whatever the source, sanction or domain--divine or human--of the custom may be. And for all the development of Greek religion and morality up to the fourth century hosion continues to connote generally "right", "proper", "specially approved" rather than strictly "holy"--in our sense of the word-- behavior.

The dictionary definition of hosion as 'whatever is hallowed or sanctioned by divine or natural law' introduces a seeming

1

precision which is inappropriate when we deal with notions as vague and wide in scope as the Greek hosion and its cognates. To begin with, "law" in any strict sense is much too precise and definite a term to cover all that traditional belief, custom and convention, transmitted by word of mouth or writing, for the most part by poets rather than legislators, decreed to be "holy". And "divine" as distinguished from "natural" or even "human" law connotes further distinctions that do not strictly apply here. For in the popular conception "divine" law and order was more synonymous with the "natural", i.e. eternal, necessary, unwritten yet inviolable order of things which men could not ignore without inevitably coming to harm than it was distinguished from it, and the crimes committed against "divine" law were at the same time the most "unnatural" acts conceivable. Furthermore, since not surprisingly it was precisely such unholy and unnatural acts that were most strongly forbidden by human law and custom, the contrast between "divine/natural" and "human/conventional" law or order could not be clearly drawn. Such distinctions, however intuitively plausible or even self-evident they may seem to us, become extremely problematic in the context of Greek popular religion and morality.[2] It is not that a designation of holiness as a religious virtue, and a specification of holy acts and things as involving our relationship to the gods, are wrong. They are merely uninformative because the modern dichotomies—religious vs. secular; divine vs. human ordinance; god-related vs. men-related conduct—are anachronistic when applied to popular belief in the fifth century and are consequently useless for its clarification.

And so are in fact most of the terms we might use to define holiness or piety by way of drawing strict boundaries between this virtue and others; the more precise and limited the scope of our terms the more unhelpful they become in an attempt to convey the almost unlimited and indefinitely extendable meaning-in-use of the Greek eusebeia and hosiotes.[3] The most cursory survey of what the Greeks at one time or other considered pious or holy reveals that, for all verbal distinctions between piety and the other traditional cardinal virtues, Greek usage failed to establish strict dividing lines between pious or holy acts and things on the one hand and those commended under the name of other, seemingly distinct, virtues.

Desecration of religious shrines, profanation of the mysteries, outright religious innovation, and any violation or even neglect of religious rites were, of course, considered unholy, but so were mistreating guests, heralds, suppliants; the young, the weak and the helpless; faithful allies and defeated enemies—or procuring free Athenian women for sexual intercourse outside marriage. Irreverence toward the gods was impious, but so was irreverence toward the dead, toward parents, elders, and a great many other members of the community. Murder, incest, and any type of blood-guilt and blood-pollution were most unholy, but so was any act gravely injurious to the community's welfare. Eusebeia required respect for whatever was "dear to the city"[4] no less than whatever was dear to the gods, and wrongdoing toward one's country was just as much an act of asebeia as wrongdoing toward the gods and daimons.[5] What all these things considered impious had in common beside being strongly disapproved of and regarded to be vicious by the community is hard to see.

The Euthyphro's and other Platonic dialogues' extremely close association, at times amounting to outright identification, of holiness and justice[6] was not Plato's own invention. It was a thoroughly orthodox association, as was indeed the linking of holiness with just about any traditional virtue.[7] For all practical purposes the notion of the "unity of virtues", explicitly argued for in several Platonic dialogues, was already implicit, albeit in a vague and not altogether coherent form, in traditional popular belief.[8]

The reason for this is not hard to find. One of the Greek gods' primary functions has ever been the sanctioning of whatever rules were regarded to be especially necessary for the orderly functioning of human society. Whether this role of the gods was merely implicit in religious belief and practice or explicitly recognized, in Greek popular morality religion always remained woven into the fabric of society and could not be separated from it without unravelling the whole. Consequently, for the orthodox, traditionally virtuous majority there could be no such thing as a strictly and exclusively religious, as distinguished from nonreligious, virtue.

Since the gods were the gods of the city, any public offense against them was at the same time an offense against the city, and any grave civic offense constituted an offense against them as the city's guardians. Since the gods sanctioned the city's laws—many, and at times all, of which were considered the products of divine legislation—while the city's laws in their turn regulated and enforced religious practices, the Pythia's counsel "act in accordance with the laws of your city and you will act piously" could be regarded a universal rule.[10] Athene was as much a symbolic embodiment of Athens as Athens was a concrete embodiment of Athene. The goddess and the city mutually supported and gave meaning to each other's existence; therefore any un-Athenian activity was eo ipso impious.

This coincidence of Athenian piety and patriotism was reinforced and accounted for in manifold ways, of which I will mention but two; one a legal measure, the other a philosophical argument.

3

Since by taking an oath a man invokes the gods and binds himself under their authority and power, oathbreaking was a direct offense against the gods. But as on attaining maturity every Athenian swore an oath of allegiance to Athens, all unpatriotic, un-Athenian behavior amounted to oathbreaking and thus impiety--as did all failure to perform the duties and fulfill the obligations anyone has sworn to perform and fulfill on entering an office, a contract, or any process regulated by law.

Reverence toward one's parents was an extremely important part of eusebeia; acts of filial piety were regarded especially dear to the gods. But the traditional notion of filial piety could be easily extended--as Socrates extends it in the Crito--to the city itself as the true begetter, nurturer and educator of every citizen, holier, more precious and more to be revered than any mere father or mother, so that injuries inflicted on law and state become even unholier than any harm done to mere natural parents. Whether or not the average citizen would understand the philosophic argument justifying such extension, he would intuitively approve of the analogy[12] and accept the conclusion which merely articulates and makes explicit his own traditional, for the most part unquestioned and unarticulated, belief. And these particular links--oaths, the extension of filial piety--used to connect piety and patriotism were but a few visible parts of an invisible chain that Greek tradition forged to make the bond between religious and civic virtue unbreakable.

Similar bonds existed between religion and any other part of Greek popular morality. Sophronein, sane thinking, the type of thought that saves rather than corrupts and destroys individual and city alike, was as much as pious as piety was wise.[13] Courage in the service of one's country--and its gods--was just as much a religious virtue as it was a patriotic as well as manly, warlike excellence.[14] As Dover sums up: "the consequence of the tendency towards identification of the patriotic, law-abiding, and the pious is that it becomes difficult to think of any conduct which could attract any kind of 'secular' valuation and yet could not be called 'pious' or 'impious'".[15] Being pious and being good were, for all practical purposes, often just about synonymous terms.[16]

The most elementary fact about Greek popular religion, almost universally noted by scholars, is its totalitarian character: religion pervaded every sphere and was involved in every aspect of the citizen's entire life. Greek religion "was from the beginning a religion of the community"[17] rather than an affair of the private individual; it was concerned with the citizens' public interaction rather than the solitary man's inward belief; and it was bound up with the state rather than being an independent institution capable of asserting itself against it.[18]

4

Religious beliefs were the foundation of the city and the city
safe-guarded, controlled and regulated religion; "state and religion were one".[19] As Murray remarks, "the real religion of the
fifth century was...a devotion to the city itself".[20] Greek popular belief would have regarded the modern alternatives irreligious as well as absurd.[21]

That is why most of Euthyphro's difficulties in providing a
precise and coherent definition of piety in the dialogue are not
of his own making; they are inherent in the tradition of which he
is but a spokesman. His assertions that piety consists in doing
what is dear to, loved by, concerned with, and performed in the
service of the gods are correct but uninformative, because in the
traditional conception of the gods such seemingly exclusive qual-
ifications--as dear to etc. the gods--in fact exclude nothing that
might be strongly approved of by the community. His abortive attempts to establish a distinction between holiness and justice
fail because they are informed by a tradition in which such clear-
cut distinctions do not exist. And not only is the obvious incoherence and internal conflict of the multiplicity of "holy" acts
performed in accordance with the will of the various gods and of
the city inherent in the traditional concept of holiness itself,
but Euthyphro's inability to resolve this conflict also stems
from his by and large uncritical acceptance of and reliance on
tradition.

The late fifth-century concepts of holiness or piety, as
well as of all other virtues, were the product of a long historical development--poetic-mythological, legal-political, moral-
philosophical--that had brought forth an amalgam of elements superficially combined but often fundamentally irreconcilable. And
the hidden tension between these elements could not help being
disclosed as the rational demand for coherent critical thought--
as opposed to mere traditional belief--grew stronger in the
course of the last three centuries.

The vast array of mythological deities, still very much a
part of popular belief, was more and more clearly perceived to be
hopelessly divided against itself. What one god arbitrarily demanded another equally forcefully and arbitrarily forbade. What
the old, chthonic gods of the blood-law insisted upon as their
due was anathema to the new, gentler, wiser and more rational
gods of civic law and civilized arbitration. And both groups of
gods were deeply opposed to all that Dionysus, the mad dissolver
of chthonic as well as civic law ever represented. If any god's
love made an act eo ipso holy it would be hard to find a single
irretrievably unholy act. If all the gods' unanimous agreement
alone hallowed an act then the class of holy acts became a null-
class.

5

Even when the principles the various gods individually stood for were not in themselves contradictory, they often clashed with one another--or indeed each with itself--when men attempted to live up to them. Not only might an act performed in the service of one god under a law still universally regarded as holy be an offense to another god and a law held in equally high esteem-- Agamemnon's dilemma in the Agamemnon--but the very principle of chtonic justice (blood for blood) became incoherent with itself (purification of blood-pollution by bloodshed causing further blood-pollution) when put into practice by men.22 Instances of pious yet inevitably impious, innocent yet necessarily guilty, wholesome yet at the same time corrupt and destructive acts multiplied, and the notion of a holy crime threatened to become common-place.23 And there was nothing that the traditional concept of holiness enabled the believer to do to avoid such contradictions. As a result the very notion of the gods being just and even holy--awesome, wholesome and most worthy of respect--came under increasing attack.24

But the growing emphasis on human rather than divine law and justice in no way alleviated the problem. For the things the city held dear, whether or not they were still thought of as also loved by the gods, were as various, changing and ultimately incoherent with each other as those dear to the gods were before. By the end of the fifth century the wide variety of conflicting laws and customs in different cities, as well as the rapid, seemingly arbitrary changes within the same city's laws and customs, made the incoherence of conventional law no less evident to those who cared to think about these matters than was the incoherence of divine legislation to its thoughtful critics. Reflection cast doubt on the divine, natural, as well as the rational foundation of any and all civil law. The nature-convention controversy, the chief intellectual battle-ground of fifth century Greece, put in question both what the gods and what the cities demanded, struck at the roots of all conventional religious, moral, as well as political belief, and threatened to undermine the whole traditional foundation of communal life.

Since the rational demand for an internally coherent and demonstrably just conception of divinity was one that the traditional willful, power-and honor-bent, anthropomorphic gods of myth were manifestly incapable of fulfilling, all attempts to rationalize Greek popular religion could only lead to its weakening. Whether undertaken in a friendly spirit and aimed at the purification and revitalization of the gods, or performed with the express aim of overcoming religion, such attempts necessarily led to a demythologizing and secularizing of religion that tended to deprive it of its traditional content and diminish its role in the city's life. But conventional justice could withstand the same criticisms no better, and offering no real substitute for

6

religion could not alleviate the problems traditional religion
was incapable of resolving.

Consequently, whatever form religious reform took in the
hands of religion's critics and defenders, and however loud the
doubts voiced were concerning the authority, power, and justice
of the gods as well as of the city, the Homeric gods in their intimate relation to the city managed to survive, and the city and
its gods continued to command the allegiance of the not too
thoughtful, conventionally pious majority of the populace. Religious orthodoxy and religious scepticism, almost blind belief
in and outright denial of the gods, stubborn resistance to change
and far-reaching religious and anti-religious innovation existed
side by side and the resulting tension threatened to tear the
community apart.

It is important to keep this in mind when we confront Socrates at the king archon's court. For the conceptual unclarity
and theoretical and practical incoherence that characterized the
Greeks' use of religious and moral terms, and the concomitant
confusion, tension and conflict that threatened Athens' entire
religious, moral and political life, not only led to Socrates'
eventual conviction for impiety; they also motivated his whole
life's activity, which in turn made his trial and conviction just
about inevitable. It was the moral-religious-political confusion
and disorientation of his city, and indeed of contemporary Greece,
that Socrates tried to alleviate by his attempts at clarifying
the meaning of such fundamental yet obscurely and incoherently
used terms as piety and justice. And it was the Athenian majority's thoughtless adherence to their conflict-ridden tradition that
made them perceive Socrates' demand for disambiguating and ra-
tionalizing their morality a kind of religious innovation that
bordered on or even constituted impiety.

Notwithstanding the fictional nature of Plato's dialogue,
reading the Euthyphro one reads what amounts to real historical
drama. Socrates' personal crisis was merely the final outcome
and most obvious manifestation of a deep-seated moral crisis that
affected every sphere of late fifth century Athenian life. It
was this crisis that Socrates sought to overcome on his own as
well as on the city's and indeed mankind's behalf. It was Socrates' solution to this crisis that brought him into conflict with
the city he was trying to save. And it was the city's sore need
for this solution--its almost irremediable ignorance of the true
bases of morality and religion--that led to its putting Socrates, its would be healer, to death.

Notes

1. On this, and the subject of this section in general, see

7

Bolkestein, _Hosios en Eusebes_ (Full titles of works referred to in an abbreviated form here are given in the Bibliography). Although this book came to my attention too late to be used extensively in these notes, I would like to refer the reader to it as probably the most useful work on the concepts of piety and holiness.

2. In spite of their being ostensibly implied by formulaic phrases like "fearing neither divine nor human laws" or "respecting sacred rights, both divine and human". Such phrases, which for the most part conjoined rather than sought to separate the two, involved verbal distinctions rather than substantial ones which popular belief would have been hard put to justify.

3. Although Rudhardt, "La définition..." pp. 102-105, argues against Caillemer, Thalheim and Lipsius who find the concept of piety elastic, indefinite and extendable, his argument concerns the legal rather than moral use of _asebeia_. And it is doubtful that his argument is tenable even with reference to the legal use of the term. For while the second part of Diopeithes' decree, e.g., was precise, the first part--ta theia me nomizein--could mean just about anything as is shown by the charges against Pheidias and Aspasia who were prosecuted under this decree. See Schachermeyr, "Religionspolitik..." p. 63; also the discussion of _nomizein_ in Fahr, _Theous Nomizein_, p. 163 et passim.

4. Sophocles, _Oedipus at Col._ 87.

5. Psuedo-Aristotle, _de virtut. et vit._ 7, 1251a31.

6. E.g. _Laches_ 199D, _Crito_ 54B, _Prot._ 330C, _Gorg._ 507A.

7. E.g. _eusebeia_ and _dikaiosune_ in Orphic Hymns prologue pros mousaion 14; _sophronein_ and _eusebein_ in Soph. _Electra_ 308, 464; _dike_, _eusebeia_ and _promethia_ in Eur. _Iph. in Tauris_ 1202; _eusebeia_ and _phren agatha_ in Eur. _Hipp._ 1419; _hosia_ and _themis_ in Eur. _Helen_ 1353.

8. See Theognis 145ff.

9. See Demosthenes 25.5. Even when civic arbitration replaces chthonic justice in the _Eumenides_ it is given divine sanction by Athene bringing about the change and the "new gods" arguing for the new way of proceeding. In fact, even when Critias makes this role of the gods explicit he does not disapprove of using what he calls the "pleasantest of lies."

10. Though Xenophon himself (_Mem._ I, 3.1) seems to subsume only matters pertaining to "the gods and the concerns of heaven" under the Pythia's rule.

11. Crito 50D - 51E. See also Demosthenes 28, 205; "everyone considered that he was born not to his father and mother alone but to his country".

12. Which Plato frequently uses (e.g. Euth. 2C; Rep. 414E, 575D) but has not invented. See e.g. Aes. Septem 16.

13. See e.g. Soph. El. 308, 464; and Critias 4, 20-21 in Diehl, Anth. Lyr. Gr. Leipzig 1954.

14. E.g. Thuc. II, 54.

15. Dover, Greek Popular Morality p. 252. My indebtedness to Dover in the preceding is greater than can be indicated by individual footnotes.

16. As were being no good, worthless (poneros) and impious. See e.g. Aristotle, Eth. Nic. 1122a6 and Pseudo Demosthenes 59.82. It is instructive to read the latter's speech against Neaira (59), a speech delivered in an ostensibly civil case yet replete with charges of impiety. The accuser plainly regards all dishonorable, lawless, loathsome conduct as impious at the same time.

17. Nilsson, History p. 232.

18. Nilsson, Geschichte p. 847.

19. Nilsson, History p. 242.

20. Murray, Five Stages p. 98.

21. On the unity of religion and state see also Platner, Processe und Klagen II, p. 138FF.; Derenne, Les Procès p. 257; Murray, Five Stages p. 106; Chroust, Socrates, Man and Myth London 1957 p. 49; Jaeger Paideia II p. 95; N.R.E. Fischer, Social Values in Classical Athens London 1976 p. ix; W. Nestle, Griechische Religiositaet vom Zeitalter des Perikles bis auf Aristoteles Berlin 1933 p. 9ff.

22. See my Man's Measure, chapter on Oresteia.

23. See e.g. Soph. Ant. 74, 924; El. 221ff., 307-9, 1095-97; Trach. 1245; Eur. Or. 546ff.; Bacch. 113-4.

24. As e.g. in Soph. Philoct. 451-2, or the concluding lines of Trach.

PHILOSOPHICAL PRESUPPOSITIONS

The concluding remarks in the previous section, concerning Socrates' motivation and purpose in the Euthyphro and the importance of his inquiry into the problem raised therein, are purely preliminary. They are to be amplified and justified by the interpretation that follows. Still, in view of the fact that there is no agreement among scholars either about the philosophical purpose of the dialogue or about what if any answers the Euthyphro provides to the questions it raises, it might be useful here to say something about the philosophical presuppositions of the following interpretation.

By and large Euthyphro-interpretations, from Schleiermacher's (1804) to Allen's (1970), can be grouped in two seemingly antithetical yet in a way complementary categories. On the one hand there are those which deny that the dialogue comes to or even provides a clue for finding a positive definition of piety[1] and conclude either that the dialogue has little merit[2] or that its merit lies in raising logical, epistemological and metaphysical problems rather than settling ethical or theological ones.[3] On the other there are the ones which do find positive answers and substantive moral theory, or at least indications of such, in the dialogue, yet do so only by interpreting the Euthyphro on the basis of Plato's later doctrines gathered from such diverse sources as the Republic, Timaeus, Theaetetus, Philebus, Laws and Epinomis.[4]

The two groups of interpretation, albeit opposed, are nevertheless complementary in that they agree that the Euthyphro, either on its own or in the context of the other early dialogues alone, provides neither an answer nor a sufficient clue to an answer to the question "what is piety?"[5] Since I disagree with this thesis that the opponents seem to share and think it possible to steer a middle course between these extremes, I would like to indicate the principles that will guide the following interpretation.

Against the positivists who rely on ethical or metaphysical theories culled from dialogues written decades after the Euthyphro, theories which Socrates is unlikely to have held and which Plato himself may not even have conceived at the time he wrote the Euthyphro, I would insist on interpreting the Euthyphro in the context of the early, Socratic dialogues only; dialogues with which it has a great deal in common both formally and materially, and which are generally recognized as belonging to that stage of Plato's work where, if at all, he is most likely to have expressed Socrates' own thought.[6] Should such an interpretation yield positive results it would establish the integrity and significance of the dialogue, which is something no positivist

11

proceeding the way described can hope to do.

Against the negativists I would argue that the dialogue requires constructive interpretation rather than the adoption of a method of approach which, if strictly observed, makes all coherent interpretation impossible and necessarily leads to purely negative conclusions with regard to the substantive content of the Euthyphro. What this type of "constructive" interpretation involves can be clarified by contrasting it with the "analytic" method adopted, at least in principle, by Allen.[7]

In the only book-length study of the Euthyphro written in the last fifty years Allen takes a stand against what he calls "interpretation in the grander sense" and quotes Grote who "over a hundred years ago gave what I take to be the true view of the dialogue:

...Socrates appears in his received character as confessing ignorance, soliciting instruction, and exposing inconsistencies and contradictions in what is given him for instruction. We must....take this ignorance on the part of Socrates not as assumed, but as very real. In no part of the Platonic writings do we find any tenable definition of the Holy and the Unholy, such as is here demanded of Euthyphro. The talent of Socrates consists in exposing bad definitions, not in providing good ones.

The search for definition in the Euthyphro (Allen continues) ends in failure. The dialogue does not say what holiness is, or what religion ought to be, and if Plato had views on either of these subjects, he has not here told us what they are. There has been no drought of critics willing to make good the omission for him; but their speculations testify mainly to the inveterate scholarly habit of finding doctrine where Plato offered dialectic. The Euthyphro, if it suggests much, concludes little. It is an exercise in dialectic, and it is as dialectic that it must be understood."[8]

"The Euthyphro ends in failure: no definition of holiness is stated, and none is implied. There is no 'mask' which can be stripped off the dialogue to reveal its true meaning; it bears its meaning on its face....The interest of the dialogue does not lie in the product of its dialectic, for there is no product; it lies in the dialectic itself."[9]

Though I do not fundamentally disagree with all that Allen says here, it is important to specify the extent of my agreement and disagreement on method and my reasons for departing from the principles of interpretation which at least ostensibly he adopts.[10]

12

To begin with, I would insist on reading Socrates' "confession of ignorance" in the Euthyphro and the other early Platonic dialogues as an ironical statement. For taking it at face value, and allowing the ostensibly negative conclusion of the dialogue to stand as proof of this assessment, would not only make it impossible to find any substantive ethical theory in any of the Socratic dialogues up to the Republic (and inclusive of Republic Bk I) but it would make the Socratic method, i.e. the dialectic itself that Allen and others claim to appreciate and regard Socrates' crowning achievement, and indeed Socrates' entire philosophical activity, incoherent and philosophically indefensible.

The Socratic profession of ignorance is a characteristic mark of all the early and early-middle dialogues. It extends to every virtue discussed and, strictly speaking, contradicts even the few positive assertions Socrates on rare occasions claims to make with confidence. Taken at face value, Socrates' profession of ignorance and the aporetic ending of all these dialogues would make it impossible to attribute to Socrates any positive views not only on the subject of holiness but on the subject of any virtue, thereby depriving the first ethical philosopher of any theory concerning human nature and human existence.

And that is not all. The Socratic claim of ignorance is, in its implications, a substantially self-referential claim which, if taken literally, makes all positive appraisal of the dialectic as a preferred method for gaining knowledge, as well as all claims concerning the value of knowledge itself, thoroughly untenable.

If after a lifetime of reflective, critical inquiry Socrates is indeed as ignorant and lacking in substantive knowledge with regard to all the issues he never ceases to raise as he claims to be in the early Platonic dialogues, how could he confidently affirm--as he does e.g. in the Meno--the worth of critical inquiry? His own utter failure to achieve the knowledge he sought for would put any faith in the efficacy of critical reflection into the gravest doubt.

If all Socrates had at the end of his life was an unjustified faith in the dialectic, what difference was there between him and his interlocutors--and indeed the Athenian masses--whose unjustified and philosophically ungrounded faith--in whatever they believed--he never ceased to criticize? If all Socrates "knew" was his own ignorance, and if this knowledge, and the consequent search for knowledge that it might inspire, were as incapable of leading to any further knowledge as they are said to have been in Socrates' case, then what are such awareness of ignorance and such search for knowledge themselves good for? And why should they make Socrates believe that he was better off-- even by ever so little; even if only by virtue of his knowledge

13

of his own ignorance—than anyone else?

And if Socrates still knew nothing of impiety—or any other virtue—at the time of his trial, how could he so confidently confront his judges and defend his whole life's activity as neither impious nor lacking in any other virtue that constituted true rather than illusory human excellence? And how could he insist on his own judgment against that of his accusers, judges and the city itself, when strictly speaking he knew nothing about the whole matter—unlike his opponents who at least believed that they knew and thus, for all their ignorance of their lack of knowledge, were at least logically consistent in having confidence in their own judgment?[11]

Even if the Socratic profession of ignorance were not logically self-refuting it would be practically self-refuting in the sense that, taken at face value, it makes Socrates' lifelong activity—the search for knowledge itself—self-contradictory: its sole basis becomes the type of rationally unjustified faith that it—the search for knowledge—is designed to overcome.

Taking Socrates' pretended _aporiai_ literally we could not even attribute to Socrates what is commonly and justifiably considered to be the cornerstone of his whole philosophy, that virtue is knowledge and that therefore the unexamined life, the life lacking in the critical reflection which alone leads to knowledge, is not worth living.[12] For in the Meno e.g. Socrates claims not to know, and never to have met anyone who knew, what virtue is, and the hypothetical argument identifying virtue and knowledge is contradicted by the immediately following, and in itself extremely paradoxical concluding portion of the dialogue which denies the necessity of knowledge for the acquisition and possession of virtue. But if knowledge is not virtue, of what virtue is knowledge itself (provided it could be gained in some manner as yet unknown to us, since, in accordance with the previous arguments the dialectic seems to be of little utility for gaining it)?

There is not the slightest indication in any of the early dialogues that Socrates considered knowledge, or anything else, "good in itself" regardless of its effect on the possessor and its contribution to the betterment of human life. On the contrary, he repeatedly disclaims—and if we take him literally we ought to pay attention to his explicit statements at least—any interest in useless knowledge,[13] and the notion of an ethically disinterested inquiry runs counter to everything we have any right to claim we know about his thinking. If knowledge is no virtue—in the strict sense of something that necessarily improves a man's life—then the practical, moral necessity of the search for it can no longer be asserted, and the very inquiry Socrates

14

undertakes in the Euthyphro and the other early and middle dialogues becomes incoherent with itself. (Indeed Socrates' whole
philosophy, whatever is still left of it, becomes absurd).

To view the dialectic as the crowning glory of Socratic activity and at the same time to accept the Socratic profession of
ignorance at face value--as Allen and his companions do--seems to
me a hopelessly contradictory enterprise. Either one must deny
the utility and importance--ultimately for the conduct of human
life--of the Socratic method itself, or one must justify one's
high appraisal of the formal, dialectical, analytic elements of
Socrates' philosophy on the basis of Socrates' substantive theory
of human life and his substantive conception of virtue as knowledge. If the dialectic has no product[14] then it is an unproductive and ultimately useless enterprise, and Socrates' claim that
the life without dialectic reflection, the unexamined life, is
not worth living must be rejected as groundless. (In this connection it is interesting to note that for Allen virtue itself
has no product or proper function, and is therefore as useless as
the dialectic "if usefulness is to be defined in terms of a concrete product or ergon, such as health or victory..."[15] What
Allen conveniently ignores here--in reference to Euthyphro 13D-
14C, and the Charmides, Republic, and Gorgias passages he cites
in support of his argument--is that the product of virtue--qua
wisdom, knowledge of good and evil--is, of course, no particular
thing or possession such as other arts produce but eudaimonia,
the overall mental-spiritual health, well-being, self-fulfillment,
happiness of the possessor. This is what makes virtue virtue--
arete, human excellence as such--that its possession necessarily
leads to and guarantees happiness, its end product, while the
possession of any other type of thing, skill, or knowledge by itself fails to do so and therefore cannot qualify as human excellence.)

This is not to say, of course, that the product of the dialectic has to be an explicit definition, clearly stated at the
end of every dialogue, of the virtue that is the subject of the
dialectic inquiry. No early Socratic dialogue of Plato ever concludes by providing such uncontroverted and immediately acceptable
definition. But the reason for the aporiai with which these
dialogues invariably end lies once again in the substantive
theories of knowledge and of virtue that justify the Socratic
method itself.

If knowledge is distinguished from opinion,[16] right or
wrong, by the manner of its acquisition, i.e. by its not being
uncritically accepted on the basis of someone else's presumed
authority but appropriated by one's own critical, reflective in-
quiry--the dialectic search that the Socratic elenchus is aimed
at initiating in the hitherto uncritical interlocutor's soul--

then providing positive answers and definitions at the end of a Socratic dialogue would be clearly counterproductive. It would merely replace one opinion with another in the learner's soul. But if knowledge alone guarantees virtue, while opinion, even right opinion, is an incomparably less reliable and usable, and therefore extremely precarious and potentially harmful guide for human life, then clearly the Socratic method that aims at turning the man of opinion into a man of knowledge must be negative. It must merely put in doubt the uncritical beliefs of the interlocutor and never provide explicitly the answers themselves that would resolve such doubts. Only then will it necessarily—since the end of the search (the excellent life) is something every rational being by nature desires—engage the learner in the process of inquiry which the dialogue itself represents and which alone can result in the type of knowledge (of the good) that is virtue.

But this means that the proper response to the Socratic inquiry undertaken in this and all other early Platonic dialogues is precisely the continuation of the inquiry that constitutes the dialogue's own substance. An interpretation of the Euthyphro that stops by merely noting its negative conclusion and accepts the final aporia as something that puts an end to the substantive inquiry fails to do justice to what is most essential in the dialogue and thereby inevitably fails as an interpretation.

A constructive interpretation, such as the very nature of the Socratic dialogue requires, does not cease to be analytic and become a kind of free floating speculation unconnected with and unjustifiable in terms of the dialogue itself. Textual analysis aims at resolving the difficulties, solving the puzzles, and eliminating the inconsistencies that one confronts on first reading a text by clarifying the meaning of a tightly knit complex of interrelated terms and articulating the structure of the argument. But to accomplish this we have to analyze a text such as a Socratic dialogue both as to form and to content so as to unfold all the interconnected though hidden presuppositions and implicit assumptions which underlie the argument, as well as the unspoken implications of all that is actually said in the dialogue. Only this type of analysis can hope to dissolve the confusion and resolve the problems of interpretation that an unanalytic and dialectically unengaged approach to the dialogue leaves unresolved. And only such analysis engages us in the activity Socrates himself is engaged in in the dialogue: the dissolving of conceptual confusion—e.g. concerning the nature of piety—and a resolving of the problems that Euthyphro's and his contemporaries' unquestioning reliance on a tradition that they did not themselves reflectively appropriate created.

Such a method of analysis is therefore far from irresponsible. On the contrary it is the only responsible method, i.e. the only way of approach that is responsive to the demand Socrates imposes on his interlocutors and readers alike.

The sole function of Socratic thought is therapy. A therapy that is to begin with a therapy of thinking: a clearing up of confusion and eliminating of contradictions within our various, so often internally incoherent, beliefs and opinions; a conceptual clarification of the terms we use so thoughtlessly in everyday discourse. Its aim is a type of catharsis: a purification of concepts that cleanses our ignorance about the subjects under discussion.[17]

But his therapy or catharsis[18] is, for Socrates, not merely one of language and thought; it is at the same time a therapy of human conduct, and that alone justifies it in Socratic terms. Socrates is not merely seeking to resolve pseudo-problems that the careless use of metaphysical or mythological-poetic language produces. What he wants above all to resolve are real problems, problems on whose solution everything in a man's life depends. The incoherence of language and thought he strives to eliminate is far from being merely verbal; it inevitably leads to an incoherence of action and life: an incoherence of our acts and their real goals, an incoherence of our particular goals with our overall natural goal (the good life), a debilitating and corruptive incoherence and disharmony within the human soul itself as well as an equally destructive conflict and disharmony within the community.

Ignoring that it is a practical harmony of human action and thought rather than a merely verbal consistency of language-use for its own sake that is Socrates' aim, and separating the logical, linguistic, and epistemological elements in his thought from the moral and existential ones simply results in making the interpretation of the dialogue itself incoherent and thus in fact cries out for Socratic therapy.

Of course, the most important criterion of a correct interpretation is whether or not it makes coherent sense of the text interpreted. So far I have merely argued that the type of approach Allen et al. take, which accepts Socrates' profession of ignorance at face value and denies that Socrates had a substantive theory of human excellence, is inevitably incoherent in that it cannot even justify the Socratic method of inquiry itself (a method for which nevertheless these negativist interpreters have such a high regard) and thus fails to be coherent with Socrates' lifelong dialectical activity.

Whether or not the interpretation that follows actually succeeds in terms of the above criterion remains to be seen. But its success will have to be measured by whether or not it shows

17

the dialogue itself to be successful in accomplishing its according to Allen merely ostensible but in my view very real aim of helping us in the search for a definition of true piety and virtue. The fact that the real aim and end of the dialogue, and of Socrates' activity, can be ascertained only by the interpretation itself does not make the movement of interpretation a vicious circle. For not every interpretation establishes the dialogue as a philosophical masterpiece. This is amply witnessed by the many readings of the Euthyphro which conclude that the dialogue, at least on its own and in its proper context, i.e. without importing into it later Platonic doctrines, is a failure. And a failure to be sure the Euthyphro is in terms of the method these interpreters have adopted.

But I would, at least initially, regard this an argument not against the worth of the dialogue but against the appropriateness of the interpretive framework. Reading the work of one of the greatest philosophers of all time we ought at least provisorically to assume that what the man had in mind he actually accomplished, and what he did not accomplish he may never have meant to do in the first place. And that therefore the negative appraisal to which a type of interpretation leads might conceivably be turned against the interpretation itself and used as a proof of its inadequacy rather than as an indication, let alone proof, of the shortcomings of the text interpreted.

There is only one argument I would like to adduce at this stage for the correctness of the approach so far delineated, and that is a historical one which links up with what has been said in the previous section.

The method of analysis I suggest we adopt is not only coherent with Socrates' philosophical activity as exhibited in the dialogue but it alone is coherent with and fits into the historical situation in which Socrates' philosophical activity itself took place.

The deep-seated moral-intellectual confusion, conflict and disorientation of which the Athenians' use of the terms holiness and piety is merely a symptom, is itself ample proof of the urgent need for and appropriateness of the Socratic analysis of the traditional concepts of human excellence. The crisis—ethical, religious, legal, political—the Athenians were experiencing did in fact cry out for Socratic therapy. The real problems Athens was faced with but could not resolve in the latter half of the fifth century did in fact call for the Socratic problem-solving, a solving of substantial problems, which we can witness in the early Platonic dialogues. It was the confusion of the age and the ambiguity and incoherence of the tradition itself that made the Socratic attempt at disambiguating and integrating his

18

contemporaries' use of moral concepts and thereby critically appropriating and purifying traditional beliefs the foremost need of the time. Socrates' goal of making the moral-political-religious life of the Greeks once again coherent was the only goal coherent with the historical circumstances that led to its adoption. Athens itself was in need of catharsis; Socrates merely perceived this need better than anyone else, and having perceived it tried to live up to the historical demand.

Even his contemporaries' response to Socrates' activity shows that, for all their almost irremediable ignorance, Socrates' accusers and judges perceived, however dimly, the moral-political aims and implications of the Socratic inquiry. Though they could not understand his arguments and appreciate his achievement, they did see that Socrates was not merely adding another opinion, however novel, concerning the gods to the many already existing and was not merely enlarging the almost indiscriminately hospitable array of mythological deities. Had Socrates been merely another poet "making new gods"--phesi gar (Meletus) me poieten einai theōn, kai hos kainous poiounta theous...Euth. 3B--his contemporaries who have not only tolerated but approved of this type of activity in the past would have had little reason to be outraged at Socrates carrying it on. But without understanding what exactly Socrates was doing they perceived very well that he was doing something quite different from what the "other poets" practiced, and that nothing was further from his mind than continuing the traditional mytho-theopoieia. They were aware of Socrates doing something rather new; advocating an approach to moral-religious beliefs that in fact threatened traditional morality, i.e. the unquestioning, uncritical acceptance of tradition itself.[19] That is exactly why they felt threatened by Socrates but not by the tragic poets, and looked upon him with a suspicion unmatched even by their suspicion of the Sophists. For all their ignorance they understood that the Socratic innovation, unlike most of the preceding ones they were willing to accept, imposed a demand on them--a demand for moral-rational autonomy--that they could not possibly fulfill. This was the subversion--of their morality as well as their self-esteem--that they could not forgive and felt they had to react to as they did.

And this is what makes the events surrounding the trial of Socrates which the Euthyphro begins to document a real tragedy. Had Socrates been a mere logician occupied with exposing fallacies in argument, or a mere rhetorician intent on defining the meaning of words in their conventional use, or even a late Sophist revelling in eristic and antilogical disputation for its own sake--let alone a metaphysician who held strange theories about the independent, supersensible reality of something called the Forms--his trial would have been a comedy of errors, almost a farce (with the protagonist most likely escaping, in the manner of old comedy,

19

unscathed.)

Indeed the trial would, most likely, never have taken place. For who in his right mind would want to bring to court and put to death an Oxford-type philosopher--as it is fashionable today to regard Socrates to have been--who loudly proclaims, without a trace of Socratic irony, that he has nothing substantive to teach on any subject whatever, and that in his view philosophy must remain forever silent when it comes to formulating substantive ethico-religious principles? Just as our moral political system, as well as our religious institutions, can easily accommodate such philosophers, fully and rightly convinced of their moral-political-religious irrelevance, the Athenians too could have tolerated them as at worst harmless oddities, and at best useful allies in supporting an ethico-religious tradition based on a faith totally outside of and unassailable by rational reflection.

But his contemporaries saw more clearly the direction in which Socrates' questions pointed than some of his modern interpreters do, and therefore took appropriate action in what they considered simple moral-political-religious self-defense: the defense of a tradition which for all its shortcomings they were unwilling to abandon and because of their own shortcomings they were unable to reform. I cannot help feeling that their failure--to tolerate and perhaps profit from Socratic criticism--is still of a lesser sort than that of those modern interpreters whose analysis of the Socratic dialectic makes it unthreatening at the price of making it practically irrelevant and substantially pointless. At least his contemporaries' reaction allowed Socrates to emerge from his trial as a tragic hero rather than as the perhaps pitiable victim of a comic misunderstanding.

Notes

1. See Rabinowitz' list of negativists in Phronesis 1958 p. 113 fn. 4, and in addition Grote, Plato I pp. 322-3; Gigon, "Platons Euthyphron" pp. 12-3; A. J. Stewart, Plato's Doctrine of Ideas New York 1964 p. 18; Allen, Plato's Euthyphro pp. 6, 67.

2. Gigon, e.g. finds the dialogue tortured, artificial, practically unsuccessful and lacking in organic unity. ("Platons Euthyphron" p. 37).

3. E.g. Allen p. 67.

4. See Rabinowitz' list of positivists, loc. cit. fns. 2, 3, 4, and in addition Zeller, Die Philosophie der Griechen p. 926ff.; Hoerber, "Plato's Euthyphro" p. 95ff.; as well as Rabinowitz' own interpretation.

5. A strikingly similar state of affairs characterizes all Lysis interpretations. See my "Plato's Lysis" Phronesis 1975/XX p. 185ff.

6. I will take for granted here the conventional Platonic chronology with respect to such early writings as the Euthyphro, Laches, Lysis, Charmides, Apology, Republic I and such slightly later ones as the Protagoras and the Meno.

7. I use Allen merely because he articulates the negativist view--concerning ethical substance--and at the same time practices the positivists' approach--at least as concerns epistemological doctrine--by interpreting into the Euthyphro Plato's later theories. As such he combines the two traditional approaches to the Euthyphro in one and the same interpretation.

8. Allen p. 6.

9. Allen p. 67, cf. also his "Irony and Rhetoric" p. 39.

10. I say ostensibly, for it is debatable whether Allen in fact follows the principles he proclaims. After deploring others' finding doctrine where Plato offered dialectic Allen proceeds to find a doctrine--a metaphysical theory of forms; after arguing against "constructive" interpretations which read into the dialogue what is not explicitly said there he proceeds to construct the hidden assumptions of the dialectic--the theory of forms; and after arguing against others' finding moral theory in the Euthyphro where the Platonic Socrates 'offered only dialectic', a dialectic that 'has no product', he does not hesitate to talk about Socrates' moral mission and his convictions concerning the product of the dialectic for human life: "Back of this (moral mission) was the conviction that rational reflection on moral principle...is of utmost importance in the living of a human life. The principles Socrates sought were Forms, standards fixed in the nature of things which would enable a man infallibly to judge the difference between right and wrong. Without knowledge of these principles the moral life became mere guesswork, and guesswork marked by mistake". pp. 47-8. See also p. 72 where Allen states that the Socratic dialectic is directed "not merely toward abstract understanding, but toward the right ordering of life".

11. Allen's view in "Irony and Rhetoric" that Socrates did not really deny the charges against him in the Apology does not quite jibe with Socrates' claim to be a benefactor of the city who deserves to be rewarded rather than punished for his activity.

12. A conviction which Allen himself is perfectly willing to attribute to Socrates. See above, note 10.

21

13. E.g. Charmides 166D, 171C.

14. Allen p. 67.

15. Allen p. 58.

16. Allen, in Vlastos, The Philosophy of Socrates p. 333, claims that a radical distinction between knowledge and opinion first appears in the middle rather than the early dialogues. I suppose it all depends on what one means by "radical". All I would argue is that without the distinction outlined here (and later discussed with specific reference to Euth. 5C-6E) the Euthyphro and the other Socratic dialogues fail to make sense.

17. See Meyer's comparison between the Socratic and the Wittgensteinian analyses of concepts. Unfortunately Meyer stops too soon and does not deal with the Socratic catharsis of human action and life to which all mere catharsis of concepts is but a means.

18. The relevance of terms like therapy and catharsis to the Euthyphro itself will be elaborated on in the actual discussion of the text.

19. And threatened it in a manner that mere criminal impiety, e.g. of the sort Alcibiades was accused of, did not. Alcibiades may have committed sacrilege but he did not challenge the authority of the state—the democratic majority—to decide what was and what was not truly impious. On the contrary he payed lip-service to tradition and courted public opinion even while seeking to bend both to his purposes. That is why the city could forgive him not so many years after the Sicilian expedition; he did not commit the unpardonable sin of denying its and its traditions' authority. Socrates did just that.

THE DIALOGUE

Setting the Stage (2A-5C)

2A   Euthyphro   What has happened, Socrates, to bring you
from your usual haunts in the Lyceum to
the king archon's court? Surely you do
not have a suit before the king as I do?[1]

Although Euthyphro's astonishment at seeing Socrates in court
stems from his superficial acquaintance with Socrates as a man who
is as unlikely to bring a law-suit as to be the deserving target
of one, Socrates is in fact a great deal more out of place in
court than Euthyphro is capable of realizing.[2] For the court,
like all other institutions of the city, is founded on and designed to enforce the rule of public opinion. Its authority as
well as its decisions are based on the consensus of the majority
as determined by the actual votes cast by the citizens assembled
for the purpose of ascertaining and asserting the city's will.
And Socrates' lifelong activity and philosophical purpose are
deeply antithetical to everything the court stands for.

While the court expresses and enforces the public will, Socrates insists on deciding fundamental issues by way of each individual's critical reflection. While the court's decisions are
based on opinion, Socrates insists on knowledge alone being a reliable ground for essential decisions and a safe guide for action.
While the court admits as accuser or judge any man whose sole
qualification is that he happens to be a citizen of Athens, Socrates demands as the only proper qualification for judgment a knowledge of the grave matters under discussion.

Socrates' entire argument in the Euthyphro and the other
early dialogues in fact amounts to a denial of the court's authority to make the type of judgment for which the city regards the
court, and ultimately itself, a competent judge. The Euthyphro's
demand for knowledge and rejection of traditional opinion and convention as a basis for moral-religious decisions we shall observe
as we go along, but it is important to note that the same demand
and rejection are voiced again and again in the other dialogues
that belong in the same group with the Euthyphro.

'Are you going to be guided by the opinion of the majority
rather than the judgment of those who are experts in the matter
under discussion?' Socrates asks Lysimachus and Melesias in the
Laches (184D-E).[3] Is not the improvement of the youth too important a goal and the corruption of their soul too great a risk for
the matter to be entrusted to the judgment of people lacking in
knowledge? (Lach. 185A) "Right decision--he asserts in answer
to his own rhetorical questions--requires judgment based on

knowledge rather than numbers" (<u>Lach</u>. 184E).[3]

Should we be swayed by "the power of the multitude to inflict imprisonment and death", he asks in the <u>Crito</u> (46C), or should we regard only the "judgment of the wise good and that of the unwise evil?" (47A) "...when it comes to deciding what is just and unjust, base and noble, good and evil, matters such as we are discussing now, ought we to follow and fear the opinion of the many or of the one man who has understanding?" (47C-D) "We must consider--he concludes--not what the many will say of us but only what the one who knows about what is just and unjust, and Truth itself, will say" (48A).

The issue that inevitably brings the philosopher and the court into conflict is one of autonomy versus heteronomy of judgment. The court, and every assembly of citizens gathered to legislate or judge, demands that each citizen recognize its authority as ultimate and accept its judgment as binding. Merely to question the city's decisions once the votes are counted amounts to civil disobedience, and to deny the ultimate authority of the demos is to subvert the very principle on which democratic rule-- as popularly understood--is based.

But this is precisely what Socrates' entire philosophical activity consists in: the questioning of all judgment based on anything other than the rational individual's own insight into the practical necessity, i.e. rationality, of the decision. Socratic dialectic is a demand for reasons, and an initiation of reasoning that will lead to a giving of reasons and accounting for whatever fundamental judgment a man is prepared to live by and stake his life on.

Relentlessly pursued, as it is by Socrates, this philosophical demand is antithetical not only to the authoritarian claims of the city's institutions--legal, judicial, political--narrowly conceived, but also to all that informs these institutions: the written or unwritten moral and religious tradition that guides, and is given particular expression in, whatever the institutions are and do.

As we shall see even in the <u>Euthyphro</u>--not to mention other dialogues--Socrates is as opposed to the poets' unofficial yet no less influential prescription of moral-religious standards as he is to the actual legislation and enforcement of laws by the official legislative and judicial bodies. From the point of view of philosophy all such legislation and direction of conduct is tyrannical: an imposition of standards not grounded in the only real authority Socrates recognizes, the authority of reason.

The quarrel between philosophy and poetry, that is already

fought in the early dialogues, is merely one aspect of a deeper quarrel that makes the philosopher a necessary antagonist of poet, prophet, lawyer, legislator and ruler alike, i.e. of all agents whose activity is not based on critical reflection. What Socrates takes on in this quarrel is not just particular beliefs and laws, or particular poets, sophists or legislators, but the entire tradition as such: i.e. as the unreflective transmission and acceptance of a heteronomous--rationally unappropriated--determination of conduct by those least qualified, or at least not manifestly qualified, to make such determination.

That it is this opposition and antagonism, much deeper and more fundamental than Euthyphro perceives, that makes the philosopher out of place in the court and alien to all it stands for is evident.[4] Yet paradoxically, it is precisely this opposition that brings the philosopher, involuntarily and to his inevitable misfortune, into the court that is such an alien environment for him. For the charges that Socrates does not recognize the gods the city recognizes--charges which are, as I have tried to show, at once religious and secular, moral and political--stem precisely from the city's accurate perception of Socrates' failure to recognize its ultimate authority. And this deeper charge is one that Socrates is incapable of refuting without abandoning everything that he stands for. Consequently, most of his arguments before, during, and after the trial, in the Euthyphro, Apology and the Crito, merely prove that, from the point of view of the city, he is indeed guilty as charged.

That in a deeper sense the charges of impiety and of corrupting not just the youth but the entire constitution and health of the city itself are not true, because Socrates' criticism of the city's tradition and traditional method of judgment is an instrument of healing rather than corrupting the city which in fact sorely needs such therapy, Socrates can merely assert as he does in the Apology but never prove to the court's satisfaction. For the court is a gathering of the multitude which is incapable of the type of reflection which would enable it to understand the Socratic argument (that rational reflection itself is the only true guarantee for any city's health).

Socrates knows this, of course, and at the conclusion of his trial expresses surprise not at his conviction but at the narrow margin by which he has been convicted. The Gorgias' image of a doctor tried before a jury of children on charges brought by a pastry-cook accurately conveys his assessment of his chances to vindicate himself in court. But this makes a careful reading of the Euthyphro on our part all the more important.

For here, unfettered by the constraints of court-procedure and the even more fateful constraints that the capacity of the

25

multitude to understand his real arguments and deliver a just verdict on his philosophic activity impose on him, he can argue his case in the language and manner appropriate to dealing adequately, i.e. philosophically, dialectically, with the very basis of the charges themselves, the popular conception of holiness and justice.5

In the Euthyphro, even more explicitly and unabashedly than in the Apology, Socrates turns the tables on his accusers and turns his trial into a trial of Athens and her religious, moral and political tradition itself. And although Euthyphro, Socrates' fictional, essentially well-meaning yet fundamentally unenlightened and unintelligent antagonist in the dialogue, is no more likely to understand his argument than are the actual judges in court, the multitude for whom, as we shall see, he is standing here, Socrates' argument is directed here not at Euthyphro but at the philosophic reader for whom Plato wrote the dialogue and from whom alone he can hope for a vindication of Socrates and philosophy. Here where Meletus and Euthyphro, and most of the real accusers and judges, are as out of place and as much out of their depth as Socrates is in court, Socrates can deliver his real apology.6

Notes

1. The loose translations of the text at the beginning of each of the following sections are provided for the reader's convenience. Since problems of interpretation in the Euthyphro seldom if ever hinge on the interpreters' divergent translations I found it unnecessary to try to offer translations coming as close to being literal as possible, except in the most crucial passages.

2. Cf. Apol. 17D where Socrates, never having been involved in a court case all his life, claims to be unskilled in the manner of speaking customary at court, a stranger to the proceedings almost to the point of being a foreigner.

3. Even the otherwise not too perceptive Laches perceives the difference between discussing matters in and out of court: "Of course, if we were arguing in a law court, there would be some reason (for proceeding differently); but here in a meeting like ours, why waste time adorning ourselves with empty words?" Laches 196B.

4. For the pervasive and never diminishing opposition between philosophy and public opinion—as represented by poet, sophist or legislator—in later dialogues see e.g. Prot. 347; Phdr. 260A; Rep. 492-3, 595-68. For the out of placeness of the philosopher in court see Gorg. 484ff.; Rep. 496E, 517A, Theaet. 172Cff.

5. Fox in "The Trials of Socrates" pp. 229-30 makes a similar point although he considers the Phaedo the dialogue that contains Socrates' real defense.

6. On this see R. Stark, "Platons Dialog Euthyphron" p. 246ff. We shall have occasion later to observe how much more the Apology's language and argument is suited to the multitude's comprehension than that of the Euthyphro, and to comment on Socrates' claims, in the Apology, to have been pious even in the traditional senses of the term which in the Euthyphro he criticizes.

2A-3E	Euthyphro:	Surely, you do not have a suit before the kings as I do?
	Socrates:	The Athenians call it an indictment, not a suit.
	Eu:	Has someone indicted you? For I cannot see you indicting anyone.
	So:	No, of course not.
	Eu:	Who indicted you then?
	So:	I hardly know the man, Euthyphro; he seems to be a young and unknown person by the name of Meletus. He is of the deme of Pitthus, if you can think of a Pitthian Meletus with long hair, scanty beard and a hook-nose.
	Eu:	I cannot; but what has he indicted you for?
	So:	No trivial matter, it seems to me, but one whose understanding reflects well on someone so youthful. For he says he knows how the young are corrupted and who corrupts them. I dare say he is a wise man, who having perceived that I am ignorant and a corruptor of his peers comes to the state like a child to his mother to accuse me. Of all the people concerned with public affairs he alone seems to me to begin rightly; for it is right to care for the young first so they become as good as possible, just as a good farmer tends the young plants first and then the others. And so Meletus clears the land first of us who corrupt the young shoots, as he says. After that, obviously, he will attend to the older generation and will thus bring upon the state many great benefits; at least that is the likely outcome of the beginning he has made.
	Eu:	I wish you were right, Socrates, but I fear the opposite. For he seems to me to begin by injuring the state at its very foundation in attempting to do you wrong. But tell me, what does he say you do to corrupt the young?
	So:	Strange things, or so they sound at first.

29

For he says I am a maker of gods; and because
I make new gods and do not believe in the
old ones, he indicted me on behalf of the
latter, or so he says.

Eu: I see, Socrates; it is because you talk of a
spirit coming to you all the time. So he
indicted you for being a religious innovator
and comes to court to slander you, knowing
that such slanders are well received by the
public. Why they even laugh at me as if I
were mad when I talk about the gods in the
assembly and foretell the future. And yet I
have never predicted anything that did not
come true; it is just that they are jealous
of all men like us. However, we must confront them without paying them heed.

So: My dear Euthyphro, to be laughed at is perhaps nothing to worry about. For the Athenians, it seems to me, are not terribly concerned if they consider a man clever, as
long as he does not impart his wisdom to
others. But when they believe he makes
others like himself then they get angry,
whether out of jealousy, as you say, or for
some other reason.

Eu: I am not eager to test their sentiments
toward me in regard to this.

So: Well, perhaps they think you are not prodi-
gal in this matter and have no wish to impart your wisdom. But I fear that out of
sheer good will to men I appear to them as
one who is not only extravagant in sharing
what he has to say with all men without being paid, but would even gladly pay anyone
who might be willing to listen to him. So
if they were only to laugh at me, as you say
they do at you, it would not be unpleasant
to pass the time in court in sport and
laughter; but if they are going to be serious then only prophets like you can divine
how things will end.

In a few ironical, almost banteringly light passages Plato
sets the stage for what follows by touching on the main theme of
the dialogue and establishing the contrast between Socrates and
his antagonists.

30

Young and unknown as he is, Meletus claims to know about the
grave matters at issue. He is wise where Socrates is ignorant;
indeed he is wise enough to have found out about Socrates' deplor-
able ignorance. Although Socrates' ascription of knowledge and
wisdom to Meletus is as ironical as his own profession of ignorance, his emphasis on the importance of the knowledge Meletus
claims to have is quite serious. Should anyone possess it he
would indeed be a public benefactor bringing great blessings on
the city.

For this matter of corruption is of supreme importance to
the whole community. Whoever corrupts the young—or even the old—
undermines the health of the whole community and injures the city
in a most grievous way. It is therefore altogether appropriate
that Meletus should initiate a public indictment (graphe) rather
than a private suit (dike), for Socrates' alleged wrongdoing involves public rather than private wrong. The case in question is
one of civic offense against the state and not just of personal
injury to some particular individuals.

This does not, however, make the charges any less 'religious', as it is immediately pointed out. Socrates' corruption of
the youth is specified to consist of religious innovation: making
new gods and not recognizing the old ones the city recognizes.
Since the gods are, as we have seen, part and parcel of the moral-
religious tradition on which the city's entire life is built, not
recognizing them threatens the very foundation of the city and is
thus inevitably both a religious and a civic-political crime. The
welfare of the community is inseparable from the integrity of its
religious beliefs.

The civic-communal aspect of Socrates' 'religious' activity
is further emphasized by Socrates drawing a contrast between
Euthyphro's and his own activity. When Euthyphro suggests it is
Socrates' talk of his private daimonion that brought the indictment on him and compares it to his own prophecies that have
brought upon him so much ridicule, Socrates demurs. Unlike
Euthyphro who has kept his wisdom to himself he, Socrates, has
cared enough for others to talk to all and sundry and would even
pay for the privilege of being listened to. And that was what
the Athenians resented: they thought he would turn others into
men like himself. Private eccentricity the city could laugh at;
public teaching, the molding of the citizens is, however, the
whole city's concern.

On this point too, Socrates has no quarrel with the city.
That teaching the young wrong ideas about what is divine—awesome
and venerable—is indeed subversive to the city's health, and
that, in general, religious, civic and moral issues are inextric-
ably intertwined, he would be the last to deny. It is merely
Meletus' and the city's application of this principle to him that

he is ready to contest.

Unfortunately Meletus' choice of a place of contest is the
opposite of the one Socrates would regard appropriate. For Meletus' claim of knowledge in fact amounts to no more than claiming
to know 'what everyone knows', i.e. what the city holds to be
holy and unholy. Fully recognizing the city's ultimate authority
in matters of belief, he naturally runs to the city like a boy
to his mother for judgment. Personally he takes nothing upon
himself; he acts on behalf of and utterly guided by the city to
which he in fact leaves all real action and decision. And that
is, of course, what Socrates is fundamentally unwilling to do.
Fully acknowledging the grave importance of these matters to the
city, but not at all recognizing the city as the ultimate authority in matters of great importance, he is as reluctant as Meletus
is eager to rely on the court's judgment. That is precisely his
crime from Meletus' and the city's point of view. And it is a
crime Socrates committed out of philanthropy, i.e. because he
cared enough about his fellow men to try to improve them and thus
benefit the whole community. Had he not attempted to heal the
city he would not now be charged with its corruption.

Ironically, Euthyphro, who is at this point as benevolent
toward Socrates as Meletus is inimical, is right in regarding
Meletus as the one who injures the city by doing Socrates wrong.
But he is right for reasons he himself knows nothing about. For,
as the next section shows, he has a great deal more in common
with Meletus and the city's orthodox would-be defenders than with
the man whom in his ignorance he is ready to defend against them.
In the manner of the impostor-heroes of Old Comedy, Euthyphro
suffers from and is a paradigmatic example of the city's own
shortcomings even while he seeks to detach himself from the rest
of the community.

3E-5C	Euthyphro:	Perhaps it will all come to nothing, Socrates, and you will conclude your case satisfactorily, just as I believe I will mine.
	Socrates:	And what is your case Euthyphro? Are you defending or prosecuting?
	Eu:	Prosecuting.
	So:	Whom?
	Eu:	A man whom I am thought mad to prosecute.
	So:	Why, can he fly away?
	Eu:	Not likely in his old age.
	So:	Who is he then?
	Eu:	My father.
	So:	Your father!
	Eu:	Yes, indeed.
	So:	But what is the charge?
	Eu:	Murder, Socrates.
	So:	Heracles, Euthyphro, most people do not know what is right and proper, for I do not think one could proceed in this matter correctly without being far advanced in wisdom.
	Eu:	Far indeed, Socrates, by god.
	So:	Is it a kinsman your father killed? Obviously it must be, for you would not charge him with murder on someone else's account.
	Eu:	But Socrates, it is absurd to think it makes a difference whether the man killed was a kinsman or not. The only thing that matters is whether the killer acted justly or unjustly; if justly, let him be, if unjustly, proceed against him though he share your hearth and table. For the pollution is the same, as long as you knowingly associate with him and do not purify yourself and him by going to court. The man who died in this case was a

33

laborer of mine who worked for us when we were farming on Naxos. One day he drank too much, got angry at one of our servants and cut his throat. So my father bound him hand and foot, threw him in some ditch, and sent a man here to ask the religious advisor what to do. In the meantime he gave little thought to the bound man and neglected him, seeing that he was a murderer and that it did not matter if he died. Which is just what happened. For he died of hunger and cold and his bonds before the messenger returned. And now my father and my relatives are annoyed with me for prosecuting my father for murder on behalf of a murderer. They say he did not kill the man, or even if he did I ought not to care about the victim seeing that he was a murderer; for it is unholy for a son to prosecute his father for murder. That is how little they know about divine matters with regard to what is holy and unholy.

So: But by god, Euthyphro, do you think you have such an exact knowledge about things divine and about what is holy and unholy that given the circumstances you describe you are not afraid of doing something unholy yourself in prosecuting your father?

Eu: I would be good for nothing, Socrates, and Euthyphro would be no different from the common multitude, if I did not have an exact knowledge of all such things.

So: Well then, my wonderful Euthyphro, the best I can do is to become your pupil and challenge Meletus even before the trial, and tell him that I have always thought it very important to know what is divine, and now that he says I do wrong by improvising and innovating in matters of divinity I have become your pupil. And "Meletus," I would say to him, "if you acknowledge Euthyphro to be an expert in these matters then you must consider me right-thinking too and must not haul me into court. And if you do not, then you must proceed against him, my teacher, rather than myself, for corrupting the old, that is me and his father; me by teaching and him by

34

admonishing and chastising." And if that
does not convince him and he does not let me
off or indict you in my place, then I will
say the same things in court that I just
said in my challenge to him.

Eu: By god, Socrates, if he tried to bring me to
court I think I would find his Achilles'
heel, and the argument in the court would be
a lot more about him than about me.

So: It is because I recognize this, my dear
friend, that I want to become your pupil;
for I see that neither Meletus nor anyone
else seems to notice you, yet he has seen
through me so sharply and easily that he has
indicted me for impiety.

The emphasis on knowledge is as strong here as in the previous section. Whereas most people might not know how to proceed
correctly in matters such as Euthyphro's action in court involves,
Euthyphro claims to be far advanced in wisdom. It is his exact
knowledge (akribos epistasthai, akribos eidenai) about divine matters, things holy and unholy, which he proudly affirms distinguishes him from the common run of men.

The knowledge Euthyphro claims to have is not some kind of
abstract, theological theory with little bearing on behavior but
wisdom informing action and leading to health rather than corruption in family and communal life. The connection between religious and civic, i.e. legal, moral, social considerations is as
pronounced here as before. What alone matters in his case is, as
Euthyphro points out, whether a man's death was brought about
justly or unjustly. If unjustly done the act inevitably sickens
all human association and pollutes the killer's social environment. The remedy for such civic pollution is purification
through legal action. The legal action is, however, at the same
time religious: the killer is brought to court under the statute
against unholiness and impiety.

Again, there is no quarrel here about the basic principles
involved; that wrongdoers must be prosecuted and pay the penalty
for their injustice everyone takes for granted, Euthyphro as well
as Socrates; indeed, as it is later affirmed (8B-E), all men and
gods alike. What is in question is solely Euthyphro's application
of the principle: whether he has a correct enough apprehension
of it to deal with the particular case.

It has been suggested[1] that the concept of pollution on which
Euthyphro seeks to base his case is too primitive, archaic and
superstitious a notion to have been taken seriously by a

reasonably enlightened fifth century Athenian such as Euthyphro—
not to speak of Socrates himself. But nothing could be further
from the truth.

In the first place Euthyphro is, as we shall see, no more enlightened than the average Athenian, and while he may be over-
zealous in his action the rules he tries to observe are thoroughly traditional and popular, i.e. still accepted by the Athenian
majority. Pollution and purification are not only prominent and
frequently pivotal problems in Greek tragedy; they are also important legal issues before and after the fifth century. Dra-
conian legislation already proscribed all association with murderers to prevent communicating their pollution to others,[2] and
charges of pollution continue to be taken quite seriously even in
fourth century court cases.[3]

Furthermore, the issue of pollution is not merely of popular
as distinguished from philosophical significance. Rightly understood, pollution remains just as serious a matter for Plato as it
is for his unenlightened contemporaries.

Ever since Solon injustice was regarded a pathological condition of the social organism; a sickness that corrupts the whole
body politic; a contagious, even hereditary, disease that undermines the health of the whole community.[4] And this is exactly
how Plato deals with it again and again in the early and middle
dialogues. In Republic I (351C-352D) e.g., injustice is said to
destroy the unity and harmonious functioning of whatever organism—individual, family, social group—it is present in, and all
through the Republic justice is viewed as guaranteeing the health
and injustice as bringing about the corruption and eventual destruction of individual and state alike. There is not the slightest indication in any of Plato's writings that he ever abandoned
this view of injustice as a kind of miasma necessarily corruptive
of the very nature of any organism.

Analogies between justice and health, injustice and disease
are prominent in the Gorgias, where legal and medical prescriptions are described as aiming at curing the organism—soul or
body—in the care of the (legal or medical) practitioner, and
saving it from the inevitable destruction its corruption is bound
to bring about (Gorg. 497-80). These analogies are especially
relevant in our context because they are used in the Gorgias to
justify, among other things, precisely the type of action
Euthyphro is engaged in here. "Should a man himself, or someone
he cares for, commit an unjust act, he must willingly go to the
judge as if to the doctor...gravely concerned lest the disease of
his injustice become a chronic and incurable infection in his
soul." "Whether it is oneself, or one's parents or friends or
children or country...a man ought to accuse himself first of all,
and then his relatives and others dear to him...and reveal rather

than conceal the injustice so as to pay the penalty and recover his health..." Whatever the penalty may be, "everyone should be the first to accuse either himself or his relatives... so that they may be relieved of the greatest evil, injustice." (Gorgias 480A-D).

That Plato is altogether earnest, even passionate, in his recommendations cannot be doubted. The principles involved, the principles under which Euthyphro claims to act, are even more rigorously and vigorously affirmed by him elsewhere than through the mouth of Euthyphro in this dialogue. Euthyphro's shortcoming is--as was Meletus' in the previous section--that he lacks the understanding which would enable him to apply correctly the principles which, however correct, are for him a matter of obscure belief rather than clear and safely usable knowledge.

However thoughtless Euthyphro himself may be, the problems he confronts in the dialogue are quite real. Plato may have invented Euthyphro's actual court-case, but he certainly did not invent the circumstances which would inevitably create precisely the type of difficulties in which Euthyphro finds himself.

Euthyphro, seeking legal-religious purification, is viewed by others as committing a deed that itself pollutes. Acting, as he believes, in strict piety in accusing his father, he is himself accused by his relatives of doing something utterly impious. Predicaments of this sort where the same act is viewed, often by the same people, as at once holy and unholy are not without reason the very stuff of fifth century tragedy; it is the state of traditional moral-religious thought that inevitably creates them. As long as the various commands and prohibitions accreted through a long historical development lack the unity and coherence that only rational reflection is capable of providing, moral-religious conflicts like that of Euthyphro--and much more serious ones like Agamemnon's, Electra's, Orestes', and Antigone's, etc.--are not only bound to occur but they remain essentially unresolvable. Agamemnon's anguished cry ti tonde aneu kakōn?--how does one choose between two equally unholy alternatives?--is bound to be heard again and again as people, trying to act in accordance with potentially conflicting laws, are themselves enmeshed in a conflict that proves fatal to them. Euthyphro may not have been serious and upright enough for this to happen to him but others were; certainly the problem was real and serious, and that is what makes Euthyphro's case representative and historically appropriate.

Speaking of tragedy, Socrates' cryptic remark in Symposium that the same man ought to be able to write both comedy and tragedy, since the knowledge required for writing either is the same, is left without elaboration there. But whatever the argument might be for proving that this is so, in the Euthyphro Plato demonstrates the close affinity of both types of drama as well as his own skill in combining the two.

Tragedies as well as comedies open the action by presenting their protagonists faced with a crisis, personal and communal, that requires resolution. The crisis is real in either case—in tragedy or comedy—but it is the protagonist's character that determines whether matters will come to a tragic or comic resolution. Protagonists nobler and possessed of greater insight than the people around them lift the action to the level of tragedy, those as bad as or worse than the multitude lower it to the level of comedy.

Euthyphro is essentially a comic figure. No matter how real his society's crisis, his comprehension of it is too shallow to see it in its true dimensions. For all his mock-heroic conflict with his contemporaries he is in fact their true representative: an exaggerated impersonation and crystallized expression of their most characteristic and most debilitating shortcomings—in this case all the basic inadequacies of their traditional, moral-religious orthodoxy. His pretended elevation above them is pure imposture and alazony: a boastful pretense to being different, an ignorant claim to know what they ignore, a holier-than-thou attitude that has no basis in reality. Sharing all their unenlightened beliefs he suffers from their basic afflictions and is part of the disease rather than the remedy.

Over against this inflated impersonation which, in the comic manner, serves to reveal Athenian religious orthodoxy in all its absurdity, we have ironic, self-deprecating Socrates laboring at deflating not just Euthyphro but, in effect, the equally inflated claims to knowledge of the Athenian public as well. Because his wisdom is by far superior to theirs and his attitude is far beyond their comprehension, his conflict with them is as real as Euthyphro's is pure imposture. Not unnaturally it is Euthyphro who survives in the drama and Socrates who ultimately does not.

Many fifth century plays, tragic or comic, care or contain a fictionalized enactment of a trial in court, and the Euthyphro resembles them in that its setting and ostensible occasion is an actual court proceeding. But, like all tragedy, the Euthyphro enacts a trial at a level much deeper than that of any actual court case: a trial that tests the strength, moral fiber and wisdom of the protagonists, a trial where the entire conduct of a man's life is up for judgment, a trial where life itself, indeed more than life, the good life, is at issue.[5] This is the trial Socrates passes in the tragic manner—his principles triumph though his life is forfeited—and Euthyphro fails comically—his conduct and all it is based on is revealed as a sham though

Euthyphro walks away unscathed.

It is, of course, no accident that so many Greek playwrights and Plato himself adopted the same theme--a moral-religious crisis of individuals and communities--for their creations. It was the same historical struggle, fought in every cultural--moral, religious, legal, political, poetic--arena that they all put on stage in an attempt to find for it a resolution.

The basic question all these dramas--tragic, comic, or philosophical--raise is the same: what are true piety, justice and wisdom? What is the safe and wholesome rather than corrupt and destructive way to live one's life? That these questions were raised with unrelenting vigor on every stage for a whole century overlapping Aeschylus' and Plato's mature lives is itself ample proof of the disorientation, loss of traditional certainty and search for new directions, that characterized this age. And this disorientation and search, that was historical rather than fictional, accounts for the form that fifth century drama as well as the early Platonic dialogues assumed. It was the only form appropriate to the content provided by history.

Aristotle's categories apply to tragic drama, and to the Euthyphro as a tragic-comic dialogue, because they apply to Athens' historical situation itself. It is late fifth century Athens that is in the grips of hamartia: a state of error and moral ignorance, in which for all their good intentions the Athenians miss the mark and fail to achieve what is good. It is the Athenians whose actions turn around and recoil on themselves--peripeteia--and bring about the opposite of what is intended--ruin rather than salvation. It is Athens that is in sore need of moral anagnorisis: a recognition of the true principles of action which traditional morality, confused, incoherent, yet tenacious and confining, failed to reveal. And, in the end, it is Athens that fails to achieve the moral catharsis that fifth century dramatists as well as the Platonic Socrates labor to bring about.

Harmartia, peripeteia, anagnorisis and catharsis are all built in features of the Socratic method as well as of classical tragedy. The Socratic dialogues start with and aim to overcome the error and confusion Socrates' interlocutors suffer from because of their ignorance of the true principles of conduct. Socratic elenchus is a homeopathic means to anagnorisis and catharsis: an intensification of the interlocutors' confusion and disorientation to the point where the absurdity and incoherence of their beliefs becomes so patent that even they--and if not they, at least the reflective reader--can no longer ignore it, so that the search for real enlightenment and the purification of their beliefs and lives can begin.

39

The Euthyphro's participants too wear masks, figurative if not real, which are even more functional than the real masks the actors wear on the stage. At the beginning the interlocutors' ostensible position is thoroughly incongruous with their real nature: Meletus and Euthyphro claim to know, Socrates to be ignorant and in need of instruction; Meletus and Euthyphro claim to purify, Socrates is accused of corrupting and subverting society. But as the dialogue proceeds all roles are reversed and all masks are torn away—at least for the thoughtful reader: Meletus and Euthyphro, and indeed the Athenian public for whom they are but masks, are shown to be impostors whose lack of knowledge leads to the corruption of the state; Socrates is revealed as the only true teacher of wisdom and purifier and healer of the community.

Plato draws the contrast between Euthyphro and Socrates in a manner well-known from tragedy. Euthyphro is as benevolent toward Socrates as Oedipus' interlocutors are toward Oedipus in OT. Yet because of his—and their—ignorance of the hero's true stature and position such benevolence amounts to nothing, and hinders rather than promotes the dramatic resolution. At the same time the contrast is also comic: Euthyphro's imposture—pretended knowledge and certainty—makes him an ally not of Socrates with whom he claims kinship but of the common run of people whom he most resembles even while professing to be most different from them.

This setting up of contrasts, real and pretended, is a dramatic device as useful for Plato as it was for the fifth century tragedians and comedians. It underscores and helps to reveal the true greatness of Socrates, and of philosophy, over against the shallowness of Euthyphro and the traditional moral-religious orthodoxy. And having set the stage Plato can now let the play, the trial, the test begin.

Notes

1. P.T. Geach, "Plato's Euthyphro: An Analysis and Commentary" Monist 50/1966 p. 370.

2. Demosthenes 20, 158.

3. See e.g. Demosthenes 21, 120 where merely to associate with a murderer—Euthyphro's father's as well as Euthyphro's own problem—is considered grievously impious; also 59, 86-7 where it is illegal to associate with someone who committed acts of "pollution and impiety", and where the polluter himself is liable to any punishment short of death, without legal redress.

4. See my Man's Measure pp. 93-4.

5. Of course, this does not set apart the Euthyphro from the

other early dialogues even though most of them have no court-setting. For what Nicias says in the <u>Laches</u> (187E-188B) about all interlocutors being put to the test and having to account for their entire life's conduct in conversation with Socrates applies to all Socratic dialogues.

5C-6E Socrates: But now, by Zeus, tell me what you claimed to know so clearly just now: what do you say is pious and impious in regard to homicide as well as all other things? Is not what is holy the same as itself in all action, and what is unholy always the opposite of the holy, like itself and characterized by a single characteristic mark as long as it is unholy?

Euthyphro: Certainly, Socrates.

So: Tell me then, what do you say is the holy and the unholy?

Eu: I say that the holy is what I am doing now: to prosecute whoever is guilty of homicide or temple-theft or any other similar offense, be he your father or mother or anyone else; and not to prosecute is unholy. And, Socrates, see what strong proof I give you that such is the law; a proof I have already given to others that it is right not to let off the impious whoever they may be. For men hold Zeus to be the most excellent and just of the gods and at the same time acknowledge that he put his father in bonds for unjustly devouring his children, and that the latter in his turn castrated his own father for similar reasons; yet they are angry with me when I proceed against my father for his wrongdoing, and so they contradict themselves in what they say in regard to the gods and me.

So: Could this be the reason, Euthyphro, why I am under indictment, that I find it difficult to accept when people tell such stories about the gods; and that is, apparently, why they say I am a wrongdoer? But now, if you who are so well informed about such matters believe them, then it seems I must agree. For what am I to say, I who acknowledge that I know nothing about them myself? But tell me, in the name of friendship, do you really believe these things happened?

Eu: Yes, and even more wondrous ones, Socrates,

43

about which most people know nothing.

So: Then you believe there really was a war between the gods, and terrible hatred and
battles and many other such things as are
told by the poets and colorfully represented
by great artists in our sacred places? The
very robe of Athene that is carried up to
the Acropolis at the Great Panathenaea is
covered with them. Are we to say that these
things are true, Euthyphro?

Eu: Not only these, Socrates, but as I just said
many others which if you wish I could tell
you about the gods and which I know will
astound you when you hear them.

So: That would not surprise me. But you shall
tell them to me at your leisure some other
time. Right now, try to tell me more clearly what I just asked you. For, my friend,
you did not enlighten me sufficiently when I
asked what holiness might be; you merely told
me that what you are doing now, prosecuting
your father for murder, happens to be holy.

Eu: And I told you the truth, Socrates.

So: But Euthyphro, you say that many other things
are also holy.

Eu: And so they are.

So: Remember then, that I did not ask you to tell
me about one or two of the many holy things,
but to let me know the characteristic mark
itself which makes all that is holy holy.
For you said that unholy things were unholy
and holy things holy by virtue of one single
characteristic. Or don't you remember?

Eu: I do.

So: Then tell me about this characteristic itself,
so that I may look to it and use it as a
standard and call whatever you do or someone
else does that is like it holy and what is
not like it unholy.

Eu: Well, if that is what you want Socrates, that

44

	is what I will do.
So:	That is exactly what I want.

The testing Socrates undertakes is a testing of Euthyphro's knowledge; "Tell me what you claimed to know so clearly". But if Euthyphro's knowledge is to be tested, it is important that the criteria for the test be given, and Socrates proceeds to delineate them. For the first time in the dialogue knowledge is not only insisted upon but it is also defined for the purpose at hand.

He who claims to know something distinctly, i.e. in such a way as to be able to recognize all its instances wherever and in whatever context they occur and distinguish them from whatever does not belong in the same class of things, must know what general distinguishing mark or universal characteristic all these instances have in common. This one, single characteristic (mia idea) must be the same in everything that is recognized as being of the same kind, for it is by virtue of possessing it that all these things are the kind of thing they are in the first place. All holy things, e.g. must have something in common, and all things that are of the opposite nature must likewise share a single form; this alone makes them, and makes them recognizable as, holy or unholy.

Since Socrates wants to use Euthyphro's definition of what is holy as a master-pattern or standard (paradeigma) that would enable him to identify all instances of what is holy, Euthyphro's giving him examples, even enumerating a great number of them, cannot serve his purpose; it cannot help him to recognize on his own and by himself instances of holiness other than the ones already given as, in spite of all their differences, identical in the relevant aspect with the ones given. The only thing that would give him this ability, to exercise independently of Euthyphro's continued guidance, would be a knowledge of what makes all instances instances of the thing in question: the eidos or idea whose possession qualifies all holy things to be called holy, and to be looked upon and dealt with in the same way (in the relevant respect).

A paradigm usable in this way, i.e. independently, by the learner himself, rather than in bondage to the teacher and guide, must be a universal standard, a concept con-ceiving, embracing, all possible exemplifications of it. It must be auto to eidos, the form itself, he mia idea, the one single characteristic trait, whose knowledge enables the knower to identify, and justify his identification of, all examples, instances and embodiments of the same form or idea.

It is important to emphasize that eidos, idea, paradeigma in the Euthyphro do not yet have all the connotations they acquire in various later dialogues. The form Socrates is looking for is not a paradigmatic instance of itself, i.e. something that looks like yet surpasses in its perfection and thus paradigmatically exemplifies, all its manifestations. The idea has no metaphysical status as some kind of reality existing independently of all its phenomenal embodiments. There is no evidence in the Euthyphro— or other early dialogues—that Socrates ever held such metaphysical theories. The sole function of the form qua paradigm is to enable us to recognize all particular instances of it whenever and wherever they occur.

Nor is there any indication in the Euthyphro that Socrates ever wanted to contemplate ideas in themselves and for their own sake, i.e. for the sake of some abstract theoretical knowledge that such contemplation might result in and which would be worth having in itself, regardless of its use in everyday existence. On the contrary, all the emphasis is laid on the practical importance of knowledge.

Even apart from the fact that what Euthyphro and Socrates are looking for here is a virtue—something that makes the possessor's life excellent—the function of all knowledge of ideas is purely practical and existential in the Euthyphro. He who knows a form (can make correct distinctions and thus) can act correctly in the area of action demarcated and clarified by such knowledge. This knowledge is not theoretical as distinguished from practical; it is both at once. Since ideas alone enable us to distinguish anything from anything else, they are what informs, guides, determines all our action. That is precisely why their clarification is all-important. The ideas we hold, clear or confused, correct or incorrect, make all the difference in our action and life.[1] And this is especially true in the case of such important ideas—ideas of human excellence—as Socrates is concerned with in this and other early dialogues.

To put the Socratic demand for the form itself, the single idea characteristic of all its manifestations, in proper perspective, we have to understand it not in terms of Plato's later theories but in relation to the theories of his immediate predecessors and elder contemporaries which provided the background and the impetus for Socrates' own philosophical activity.

The Sophists emphasized the relativity and context-dependence of our use of terms and did not believe that the tremendous multiplicity of the particular instances to which the same term was applied had any one specifiable trait in common. They perceived clearly that the same thing (e.g. killing) can have contrary characteristics (be just or unjust), and that opposite things (e.g. taking and sparing human life) might be the same in some respects (e.g. might both be just) in different contexts, depending on the person (enemy or friend; incurably diseased or healthy), the circumstance (war or peace, fatal illness or the best of health) and the manner and purpose (merciful or needlessly cruel; self-defense or wanton violence) of the actor or action involved. Despairing of the possibility of saying anything that was absolutely true in all circumstances, they gave up the attempt to provide universal definitions and confined themselves to enumerating instances and multiplying examples in an effort to make clear what they meant by the terms they used.

This is where Socrates made a significant departure from Sophistic practice and initiated a type of questioning that was all his own. While recognizing the relativity and context-dependence of discourse and thinking that the Sophists insisted upon, he argued that such relativity in no way proved or implied that the diverse and indefinitely multiple instances we designate by the same name had nothing in common. On the contrary, what relativity ruled out was precisely the enumeration of instances for the purpose of giving a definition. For clearly, the Sophists were right in affirming that no particular thing or act was always and necessarily an instance of any of the terms--good, bad; just, unjust; helpful, harmful; nourishing, debilitating--applied to it in different contexts and situations. But if such material definitions--giving particular instances--were ruled out because of their lack of universality then what we had to provide in a definition was precisely the formal characteristic that regardless of their material diversity all things of a certain kind had in common. (All things we call food, e.g. share the formal trait of being nourishing to some living organism, in spite of the fact that no particular thing is food for all.)

That contrary to the Sophists' belief there had to be such common form characteristic of all things of the same kind was plain to Socrates from the very fact that we were able to act in relation to, and speak and understand others' speech about, the things in our world. For if all instances of a given sort of thing or quality had nothing recognizable in common, how could we ever recognize anything as anything; how could the Sophists ever identify even single instances as instances of something, and what reason would men ever have for calling different things by a common name, and treat them the say way, as we in fact do? All discourse, all communication, all action rests on our ability to recognize, and classify things in accordance with, universal characteristics. Their presence, and our ability to perceive them, are necessary presuppositions of all we do or say.

If this is true then regardless of our temporary inability to specify exactly, let alone correctly, the universal characteristic all instances of a certain kind of thing we designate by a certain term share, we must nevertheless have some notion of the form in question and must be already using it in dealing with and talking about things. This notion may be vague or precise, true or false, it may be more limited or more extended than its correct application would require, but it cannot lack universality altogether.

But such hidden and often obscure possession of such notions, be they right or wrong, which is presupposed for thinking, speaking and acting at all is not yet knowledge. What is needed for turning it into knowledge is to bring them from hiddenness to light by articulating them distinctly and thus making them clear: giving them exact definition. And that is precisely what Socrates is asking Euthyphro to do.

It cannot be emphasized strongly enough that the Socratic theory of ideas in the Euthyphro, according to which an apprehension of formal notions, universal characteristics of some sort, is presupposed for all thought and discourse, does not yet carry any part of the metaphysical burden of Plato's "Theory of Ideas" as formulated in some of the later dialogues.[2] It does not assert or imply the independent reality of the Ideas or presuppose the immortality of the soul, the acquisition of ideas before birth, their forgetting consequent upon the union of soul and body, and their gradual recollection through what we call learning.

Although Socrates does not explicitly discuss the source of our ideas in the Euthyphro and the other dialogues belonging to the same period, it is clear enough where Euthyphro's ideas come from. All of Euthyphro's notions concerning holiness or piety are altogether traditional; he learned them, as he learned to speak and act, by being brought up in a society that transmitted to him and taught him to use the ideas it itself had. In acquiring his city's culture Euthyphro acquired the city's beliefs, opinions, ideas; its ways of thinking and acting. These ideas and ways in fact preexisted; but they did so in the Greek community rather than in some Platonic heaven. Communal rather than otherworldly experience is the source of these ideas which are immanent in the community rather than existing independently of it in a transcendent realm.

And this is also the source of their obscurity, imprecision and internal incoherence. Since they are inculcated in the individual who passively accepts and learns to use them as he grows up in the culture without appropriating them by his own active critical reflection, it is unlikely that they will be clear and transparent to him even though he is habitually using them. And as long as they are unclear, there is no guarantee that they will be coherent with each other. While their obscurity will hide much of their incoherence, the weight of tradition behind them will discourage the kind of critical reflection which alone might make

48

them clear and help eliminate their inconsistencies. This, after all, is what is so wrong with the purely traditional transmission of ideas, and it is this great shortcoming of orthodoxy that the Socratic questioning, the testing of traditional ideas that he is about to undertake in the Euthyphro, is designed to remedy.

Such testing by itself does not presuppose any theory about the independent reality of the ideas themselves. It is based on a minimal conception of human rationality: that reflecting on our everyday use of words, and thus on our traditional opinions and customary ways of interacting with the world, we will be able to clarify them—by gaining insight into the common characteristic each connotes—as well as their relationships to each other. Once we have done that and are able to give an account of what we in fact say and do in everyday life, we possess knowledge as distinguished from mere opinion. And possessing it will enable us to act in an informed rather than confused and unreliable way; our action and life will be as coherent and harmonious as will be the ideas that inform them. That is all there is to the Socratic theory of knowledge that is presupposed for and implicit in the Euthyphro.

In his first attempt to comply with Socrates' request for a definition of what is holy Euthyphro succeeds about as well as can be expected from a man of conventional upbringing who is unfamiliar with the Socratic method of inquiry. "I say the holy is what I am doing now: to prosecute whoever is guilty of homicide or temple-theft or any other similar offense, be he your father or mother or anyone else; and not to prosecute is unholy," (5D-E).

Euthyphro's 'definition' is in fact not as bad as some others we find in the early dialogues. For he does not stop with "what I am doing now"—merely pointing to a unique instance whose denotation is furthest removed from giving a universal definition—but provides some content to the concept of holiness by not only enumerating particular kinds of acts—homicide, temple-theft—whose prosecution he considers holy but expanding the enumeration by adding "any other similar offense". This expansion increases the scope of his definition and brings it closer to making it universal than it would be without the addition. Likewise, the addition "or anyone else" generalizes his enumeration of the persons to be prosecuted beyond the particular examples "father and mother".

Nor is that part of his "proof" where he accuses the Athenians of inconsistency in judging his and the gods' acts differently altogether unphilosophical. For all its alazony—Euthyphro setting himself on the level of the gods and demanding equal treatment—Euthyphro's demand is theoretically in line with that

of Socrates': given the holiness or unholiness of a type of ac-
tion--prosecuting wrongdoers--the particular agents involved--
men or gods--ought to make no difference; like cases ought to receive like treatment. Whatever acts have the same character in
the relevant respect--injustice--must be viewed the same way--as
to be prosecuted--in the same context--the preservation of holiness. Holiness and justice ought not to be respectors of persons.

Nevertheless, Euthyphro's 'definition' falls far short of being adequate by the Socratic criteria. To begin with, the addition "any other similar offense", though not ill-conceived as an
attempt at increasing the universality of the definition, does
not really do the job it is designed to do as long as Euthyphro
fails to define what other "similar offenses", offenses of "this
sort", might be. The enumeration of homicide and temple-theft
does not specify the relevant similarity of these and other acts;
it does not articulate the universal mark or characteristic these
acts, let alone others of "this sort", have in common, and failing that it does not really define the sort of acts in question.
Because Euthyphro neglects to specify the eidos or idea of the
type of action he means to refer to, his attempt to go beyond a
mere enumeration of instances to the type in fact accomplishes
very little. Lacking the idea--of the sort, the kind, the relevant similarity--we cannot use the instances as a paradigm in
the sense Socrates wants to use the definition, i.e. as an aid for
identifying any and all acts "of this sort".

And even if we articulated the universal characteristic of
all acts of this sort--i.e. acts to be prosecuted--that is implicit in Euthyphro's statement as "injustice" or "wrongdoing"
(adikia, hamartia 5D), our difficulties would be far from overcome. Apart from the fact that lacking a definition of what is
just or right action we would merely replace one unknown term to
be defined by another, and that the complete identification of
holiness and justice is something Euthyphro later resists (12E),
the definition would still remain inadequate by virtue of its
lack of universality. For as Socrates points out (6D) there are
many other acts besides prosecuting the unjust that Euthyphro regards holy, and so Euthyphro's statement fails to cover and thus
enable us to identify all holy acts. Not being literally conceptual enough--con-ceiving, embracing, applying to all that is to be
subsumed under the notion of holiness--by virtue of not being
sufficiently formal--expressive of the form, idea, universal
characteristic--the definition fails to define adequately.

The proof Euthyphro offers in support of his definition is
even more objectionable to Socrates than the definition itself:
"...men hold Zeus to be the most excellent and just of the gods
and at the same time acknowledge that he put his father in bonds
for unjustly" acting. Euthyphro cites divine precedents and

appeals to human convention as the ultimate proof of the correctness of his own act. That he does so is hardly surprising. The
source of his notion of holiness or piety is, as we have pointed
out, the conventional beliefs of his contemporaries, the moral-
religious tradition of his time inculcated in and unreflectively
accepted by him in the course of his conventional mythological-
poetic upbringing, and by the manner of his "proof" he demonstrates his almost total reliance on traditional custom and convention as the source and foundation of his own beliefs.

Euthyphro does not notice the inconsistency of his position:
that on the one hand he appeals to what "men believe" (nomizein)
and "agree on" (homologein) and on the other rejects some of the
things they agree on, e.g. that he is doing something impious; or
that his valid argument for such rejection--the inconsistency of
people holding the same act just and unjust in contexts that are
not relevantly different--is a rational argument whose introduc-
tion as something outweighing any and all factual agreement of
men undercuts his own appeal to precisely that agreement; or that
the apparent inconsistency of people's judgments ought to make him
suspicious of human convention and critical of rather than dependent on it.

Since all these inconsistencies are merely the result of
Euthyphro's own unreflective acceptance of the city's traditional
belief, that is where Socrates begins his attack: "...do you
really believe these things happened?" (6B); "are we to say that
these things are true?" (6C). The things to which Socrates refers
here are what according to Euthyphro "men believe" and "agree on"
(6A), the traditional stories they tell about the gods (6A),
stories of war and hatred and battles and the like among the gods
as told by the poets and represented by the painters in sacred
places and on the ceremonial robes carried at the Panathenaea, the
oldest and most important of Athenian festivals. It is the entire
mythical-ritual tradition of his city that Socrates is putting
into question.

In doing so, and in contrasting his own attitude--'somehow I
find all these stories difficult to accept' (6A)--to Euthyphro's,
Socrates in fact admits the literal truth of the charges against
himself and for all practical purposes demonstrates his guilt as
specified by Meletus' indictment. For the indictment charges
precisely that Socrates does not believe in what the city holds
to be true in matters concerning the gods and fails to accept
what the city accepts. The crime he is charged with is simply
and solely a lack of religious orthodoxy:3 just the type of un-
Athenian behavior he exhibits here in questioning and doubting
the traditional beliefs of Athens. That he claims "to know nothing" about such matters (6B) hardly mitigates his offense; from
the city's point of view this claim itself is inevitably suspect
and subversive. Every citizen "knows", i.e. has been told, and

has seen depicted everywhere, the stories about the gods; they cannot be "unknown" to any man who spent his whole life in the city as Socrates has done. Still to profess ignorance of them, as Socrates is doing, amounts to using standards of knowledge and criteria of judgment other than those the city recognizes, and to regard these as supervening the city's own. Nothing could be more subversive and destructive to tradition than this, in the city's eyes.

Socrates knows this, of course, and puts his finger on the substance of the charge against him: '...is not this the reason for my indictment that I do not accept uncritically what is transmitted by tradition? That is, it seems, why they say that I am a wrong-doer' (6A). But since this indictment is literally true in the sense in which it is understood by Meletus and the Athenian public, there is nothing Socrates can do to escape conviction in court--at least not without being evasive at best and deceitful at worst. There is, however, a great deal he can do out of court, or in the court of philosophy where his case is up for judgment here in the Euthyphro. And that is what he proceeds to do: to justify his conduct not by disproving the charges as the public understands them but by proving their understanding itself thoroughly inadequate and inappropriate to the gravity of the matter under consideration.

Before he can do that, however, Euthyphro's--and the Athenians'--notion of holiness needs to be articulated clearly enough to reveal its untenability.

Notes

1. From the very beginning of the dialogue where Socrates applauds Meletus' (2C-3A) and Euthyphro's (4E-5B) presumed possession of knowledge to the end (15E-16A) where he deplores Euthyphro's failure to instruct him, it is the practical results of the possession or lack of knowledge that Socrates emphasizes and no other results does he even mention.

2. Notably in the Phaedo. Maybe I should have put the words "Plato's Theory of Ideas" in quotation marks all along, since I do not find such a single, coherent theory embodied in Plato's dialogues. Rather, Plato's theory of knowledge seems to me in a continued process of development and to undergo a series of critical revisions and reformulations all through Plato's career. Thus to speak of a "Theory of Ideas", a single body of doctrine, in Plato confuses rather than clarifies the issue.

3. At least if the corrupting-the-youth charge is also interpreted as making the youth equally unorthodox.

6E-8B Euthyphro:	Well, then, whatever is dear to the gods is holy and whatever is not dear to them is unholy.
Socrates:	Beautiful, Euthyphro; now you have given me the kind of answer I was looking for. Whether it is true I do not yet know, but of course you will show me that what you say is true.
Eu:	Of course.
So:	Come then, let us examine what we say. Whatever thing or person is dear to the gods is holy, whatever hateful, unholy; and the two are not the same but rather the holy is the direct opposite of the unholy. Isn't that so?
Eu:	It is.
So:	And it seems to be correct?
Eu:	I think so, Socrates.
So:	But did we not also say that the gods quarrel, Euthyphro, and disagree with each other, and that there is hatred among them?
Eu:	We did.
So:	And what kind of disagreement brings about hatred and anger? Let us look at it this way: If you and I disagreed about numbers, for instance as to which is larger, would this kind of disagreement make us hateful to and angry at each other, or would we quickly settle such matters by resorting to arithmetic?
Eu:	We would.
So:	And if we disagreed about what is bigger and smaller in size, we would put an end to the disagreement by recourse to measuring?
Eu:	We would.
So:	And by recourse to weighing, I believe, we would settle questions about what is heavier

53

and lighter?

Eu: Of course.

So: What kind of disagreement, then, would we be unable to resolve so that we would end up hating each other and angry? Perhaps you do not find this an easy question, but I will make a suggestion: Is it not about what is just and what is unjust, honorable and disgraceful, and good and evil? Are not these the things which you and I and all other men cannot settle satisfactorily when we disagree about them and so become enemies when this happens?

Eu: Yes that is exactly the kind of disagreement, Socrates.

So: What about the gods, then, Euthyphro; when they disagree do they not disagree about these matters?

Eu: They do, necessarily.

So: Then according to what you say, my noble Euthyphro, different gods think different things just and unjust, honorable and disgraceful, and good and evil. For they would not quarrel with each other if they did not disagree about these matters. Is that so?

Eu: Yes.

So: And does not each of them love what he considers good and just, and hate the opposite of these?

Eu: Certainly.

So: But, as you say, the same things are considered just by some and unjust by others, and because they disagree about these things they quarrel and fight with each other. Right?

Eu: Yes.

So: If so, it seems that the same things are hated and loved by the gods, and are at the

54

	same time hateful and dear to them.
Eu:	Most likely.
So:	And the same things would be both holy and unholy, Euthyphro, by this argument.
Eu:	I dare say.
So:	Then, my excellent fellow, you did not answer what I asked. For I did not ask you what is at the same time holy and unholy, yet now it looks like what is dear to the gods is also hateful to them. And so it would not surprise me Euthyphro if what you are now doing in chastising your father were dear to Zeus but hateful to Cronus and Uranus, dear to Hephaestus but hateful to Hera, and so on with regard to any other gods if they disagree with each other about this matter.

There is a definite improvement in Euthyphro's new definition; it now has the requisite universality. Unlike the examples given before—prosecuting murderers, etc.—it presumably embraces all acts that are holy. And, unlike the previous universal yet indefinite "offenses of this sort", it attempts to specify what it is that all acts of this sort have in common: they are all dear to the gods. Nevertheless there are serious difficulties with accepting this new definition, as Socrates proceeds to point out.

To begin with, Euthyphro professed to believe the myths about divine conflicts, mutual hatred leading to actual warfare (6B), and continues to affirm the existence of quarrels and disagreements among the gods in answer to Socrates' reminder. He could hardly do otherwise and still base his case on tradition and convention; traditional myth is full of stories of this sort.

His own example, offered as proof of the justice of his case, shows, as Socrates points out, that what is dear to one god is more than likely to be hated by another—since Zeus hated while Cronus presumably loved devouring children, and Zeus loved while Cronus presumably hated the chastisement following this act. Examples of this sort could be multiplied indefinitely, as Socrates gleefully indicates, and Euthyphro who a short while ago offered to go on telling Socrates about many even stranger ones has to accept the fact.

Since the gods of traditional myth do not in fact hate and

love the same things but what is dear to one is often hateful to another, the same things turn out to be at once loved and hated by them, and thus in terms of Euthyphro's definition at once holy and unholy. But Euthyphro stipulated that what is holy is the direct opposite of what is unholy (7A), and this stipulation rules out the acceptance of the definition whose application leads to results contrary to what is stipulated.

Socrates does not stop with pointing out the incoherence of traditional myth and the incoherence of Euthyphro's own position in relying on it while attempting to formulate a viable definition. He also points to and begins to reveal the underlying cause of such incoherence.

Concerning matters decidable in terms of objective, universally agreed upon standards there is no lasting disagreement among men. Disputes about number, size, weight, and the like, are easily settled by counting, measuring and weighing. When it comes to other matters, however, such as justice, beauty, and goodness, men, and presumably the gods too, have difficulty in settling disputes and the consequent disagreement sets them against each other in unresolvable conflict.

It is important to point out[1] that Socrates is not drawing here the fact/value, description/prescription distinction so familiar in modern philosophy. On the contrary such a dichotomy is most emphatically rejected by him. Questions of 'value' are no less factual and in principle decidable for him than are questions of 'fact'. The distinction he draws here is not one between fact and value but one between knowledge and ignorance within an area or field of inquiry—be it mathematical, physical or moral—that is in principle fully capable of being governed by knowledge.

What the arts of counting and measuring have in common is that they all operate with agreed upon standards and criteria of judgment. This is what makes them technai, fields wherein knowledge rather than unsupported and unjustifiable opinion has the last word. These fields are all paradigmatic in the sense Socrates gives the word in the Euthyphro (6D-E): they operate with a standard which enables each individual to judge the questions involved on his own, without relying on anyone else's judgment. And since the paradigm used—the standard of judgment one learns in learning these sciences—is one and the same for all people, all individuals' judgments concerning all matters decidable by the use of such paradigms necessarily agree.

But this state of affairs—decidability by means of knowable standards, and thus general agreement among the knowledgeable in judging what is the case in all matters falling within the field of knowledge—is for Plato by no means confined to mathematical or scientific fields in our sense of the word. If it were, Socrates' entire line of argument in the Euthyphro--seeking knowledge, insisting on a paradigmatic definition, rejecting mere conventional prescription--would be pointless and misdirected.

We have touched upon the Platonic analogy between justice and medicine in discussing Euthyphro's concern for avoiding pollution, and emphasized that it was Euthyphro's fundamental ignorance about the meaning of the principles involved rather than the falsity of the principles themselves under which he claimed to act that was the cause of his mistaken actions. Plato's wholehearted and repeated affirmation, in the early and middle dialogues, of the validity of the analogy between medicine and justice makes it quite clear that he regards the two fields completely analogous in that they are both capable of scientific treatment, both dealing with subjects that are fully a matter of knowledge. The Socratic dictum "virtue is knowledge" would be incomprehensible if ethics was in principle less scientific than medicine or any other field of practical knowledge that is governed by knowable limits, standards, due measures and criteria of judgment.

What distinguishes the fields of judgment within which disputes do not lead to unresolvable disagreement from the fields where they often do in the Euthyphro is simply that the former require less knowledge and a lesser ability to acquire that knowledge than do the latter, and so most, possibly all, people have or can acquire the knowledge required in the former while few have either the knowledge or the ability to acquire it in the latter. And it is this lack of knowledge rather than a lack of knowability that leads to disagreement in matters of morality.

This is what Socrates argues in Republic I (349Eff.), e.g.: that people who know music, medicine or justice, and in general those who are experts in any field of knowledge, all agree in their judgments concerning matters in their respective fields. Only those lacking in knowledge disagree, with the knowers as well as among themselves, and their disagreement is the result of their ignorance of the standards, due measures, rational principles governing the particular field rather than of the absence of such standards within the field. They cannot act paradigmatically because they do not know the paradigm, the true criterion of judgment whose use would lead to universal agreement.

But this is precisely the situation of Euthyphro and his contemporaries as long as they rely on the traditional beliefs of popular morality for guiding their particular judgments. Operating with examples, historical-mythological precedents conventionally used for judging holiness and justice, and ignorant of the standards applicable to these fields, their judgments are as incoherent as are the judgments and loves and hates of the mythological gods themselves. Not being based on any knowledge of the eidos or idea, the universal characteristic mark of all just or holy acts and things, their opinions lack the only thing capable of eliminating incoherence and bringing about universal agreement. Their disagreement is thus a proof--since it is the result--of the ignorance of those making judgments rather than of the unknowability of the subject under consideration.

In the next section Euthyphro seeks to escape this implication and defend his own action as universally held to be just by finding an area of universal and necessary agreement in the moral judgments of men and gods. But his attempt fails and incoherence persists because of the reasons just discussed.

Note

1. Cf. Allen, Plato's Euthyphro pp. 32-3.

8B-9C	Euthyphro:	But I believe, Socrates, that no gods disagree with each other concerning this, that whoever kills someone unjustly ought to pay the penalty.
	Socrates:	What about men, Euthyphro; have you ever heard anyone argue that whoever killed someone unjustly, or did any other unjust deed, ought not to pay the penalty?
	Eu:	Indeed, people never stop arguing just that, in and out of court. No matter how many crimes they have committed they still do and say anything to escape the penalty.
	So:	But do they admit that they have acted unjustly, and while they admit this still say that nevertheless they ought not to be punished?
	Eu:	No, they do not do that.
	So:	So there is something they do not do or say, for they do not dare to say or argue that when they do wrong they ought not to be punished. Rather they say that they have not done wrong. Is that not so?
	Eu:	Yes it is.
	So:	Then they do not argue that the wrongdoer ought not to be punished, but more likely they dispute about who has done wrong and what has he done and when.
	Eu:	Quite.
	So:	But is not the same with the gods? If as you say they quarrel about right and wrong, do not some of them assert while others deny that an unjust act has been committed? For surely no one, no god nor man, dares to say that a wrongdoer ought not to be punished.
	Eu:	No, on the whole you are right on this point, Socrates.
	So:	Then it seems that it is particular acts that men and gods dispute about, if the gods dispute at all; they dispute about some act which

some of them assert to have been done justly, others unjustly. Is it not so?

Eu: Yes.

So: Well then, my dear Euthyphro, tell me, so that I may become wiser, what proof have you of this that all the gods regard a man to have died unjustly when, being a servant, he committed murder and was bound by the victim's master and died as a result of being bound before the man who bound him learned from the religious authorities what to do with him, and that it is right for a son to proceed on behalf of such a man against his own father and indict him for murder? Come, try to show me clearly that all the gods necessarily consider this act right, and if you succeed in showing me this I will praise you for your wisdom as long as I live.

Eu: But this is not a small task, Socrates, though I could do it.

So: I see. You think I am harder to teach than the judges; for obviously you will prove to them that these things are wrong and that all the gods hate such things.

Eu: Very clearly, Socrates, if they will only listen to me.

The logic of Socrates' argument against Euthyphro is clear. The formal premise "no man or god disagrees that the unjust must pay the penalty for their injustice", even if granted for the purposes of the discussion, is not sufficient to prove that all men and gods agree in regarding Euthyphro's action—or any particular act whatsoever—just. Material disagreement is in no way eliminated by the acceptance of the formal principle in question, for the principle by itself and without further elucidation has no bearing on and is useless for deciding what particular acts are to be subsumed under it (i.e. are unjust/punishable).

But if this principle fails to provide a usable paradigm—something that enables one to determine what is and what is not an instance of it—the question is what makes it fail in spite of its formal universality? To answer this we have to inquire into the status of the rule itself that Euthyphro and Socrates accept at the outset. Is its acceptance itself necessary?

The implication of the argument here, that since men and gods alike regard what is unjust punishable they all love what they consider just and there is no disagreement on this point among them, resembles Republic 334C^1--"It is reasonable (eikos) that everyone loves those he considers useful (chrestous) and hates those he considers worthless (ponerous)"--and similar passages in the Lysis (e.g. 210C-D) and other dialogues, but the analogy between these passages is far from complete.

The argument in the Republic is analogous in that it too proceeds to show that agreement to the principle stated does not guarantee the correct identification of the people--useful or worthless--to whom the principle applies. ("Don't men make mistakes about this, in that they consider many people useful who are not, and vice versa?") But as to the principle itself the analogy breaks down. For Socrates, here and elsewhere, regards the principle that all men love what they consider useful, beneficial or good to be necessary in terms of practical human rationality. A teleological being necessarily loves, desires, goes after what he considers good--useful, beneficial, profitable, etc.-- and hates, tries to avoid and to eliminate from his life whatever he considers to be of the opposite nature. Socrates makes the same point in the Meno (77C-78B): to desire what one considers bad, harmful, evil to oneself would mean to want to be miserable and no one can rationally desire to live miserably rather than happily. Therefore loving, desiring, wanting, going after what one considers good is common to all men by nature, and the opposite is teleologically self-contradictory: contrary to the basic practical rationality all men qua men, the wise as well as the ignorant, necessarily share.

In contrast to the rational or natural necessity of all teleological beings loving what they consider good, the agreement among gods and men that the unjust must pay penalty rests on a much weaker foundation in the Euthyphro.

To begin with, Euthyphro states only that whoever considers an act unjust necessarily considers it punishable. Although he clearly wants to use this statement as a premise to the conclusion that all--gods and men--love justice and hate injustice, the latter does not follow from the former (at least not without further premises establishing a necessary connection between what is good and what is just, what is bad and what is unjust; and these premises Euthyphro does not even articulate let alone try to establish as necessary in terms of the very nature of human practical rationality).

Then Socrates immediately weakens Euthyphro's proposition to stating not that no one ever thinks, believes, or holds but that no one ever argues (amphisbetein) that unjust acts ought to go unpunished. It is not stipulated here that there is a necessary agreement in all human thought about this matter by the very nature of our shared teleological rationality; the stipulated agreement concerns actual human behavior, public behavior as observable in court where people never argue that the unjust ought to escape punishment. It is a factual public agreement Socrates is willing to stipulate rather than a rationally necessary one. (Which does not mean, of course, that the original principle might not be, for Socrates himself, a necessary conclusion from necessary fundamental principles such as the ones discussed above).

And the conventional motivation for this agreement--in not arguing--is not, as far as specified here, the rational impossibility of presenting such arguments but simply a lack of daring on most men's part. Whether or not they in fact agree with the principle, they simply dare not (ou tolmosi 8C; oudeis tolma 8D-E) argue against it in public; literally they do not dare to stand apart (amphisbetein) from and disagree with public opinion on the matter. As Callicles points out in the Gorgias where the subject of punishing the unjust is discussed, it is "conventional" rather than natural, rationally necessary agreement that is asserted here. Far from being convinced of the rightness of the principle, people merely pay lip-service to it; in actual fact they are "ashamed and do not dare to say what they think" (482E) which is most likely the opposite of what they publicly affirm.

Of course Socrates himself does not consider the principle in question—that the unjust ought to be punished--in the Euthyphro and in the Gorgias to be true by convention rather than by nature, and repeatedly presents arguments from nature that lead to the principle as their conclusion. But the point is that Callicles is perfectly right as to the basis of Euthyphro's, and the average citizen's, affirmation of the principle. For Euthyphro cites public opinion and the behavior of men in public as proof of his statement. And it is this method of proof, i.e. Euthyphro's uncritical reliance on orthodox opinion, that makes him incapable of even attempting to prove the justice of his own case, let alone establishing the necessary agreement of all rational judgments-- of men and gods--about any and all particular instances of justice and injustice.

For had Euthyphro any idea why injustice must be punished-- e.g. because it is destructive to the community--the universal and formal principle he states would no longer be unparadigmatic; it would enable him to make particular judgments concerning what is just and unjust, and to justify them by making use of the paradigm. But that would mean that he would in fact possess the knowledge of the eidos or idea of justice and holiness which he so obviously lacks. And it is this lack of understanding rather than merely voicing the principle that makes him incapable of applying

62

it.[2] His having mere belief, uncritically accepted and regurgitated public opinion, rather than knowledge is the cause of all his difficulties, here as before.

Although neither Euthyphro nor Socrates seem to regard the statement "whoever is unjust must pay the penalty" as analytic,[3] interpreting it as tautologous the way Guardini does would lead to much the same result as outlined above. If the statement "injustice must be punished" means the same as "injustice is injustice", "whatever is unjust is unjust", i.e. if "unjust" and "to be punished" mean the same thing by definition, then the statement is utterly useless as a paradigm in the Socratic sense. Merely equating "unjust" and "punishable" it provides no information whatever as to the nature of what is unjust/punishable. An assent to it is purely verbal--an agreement to use the two terms interchangeably--and guarantees no agreement whatsoever concerning the material use of these now synonymous terms. Apart from their agreed upon synonymy the meaning of these words is left totally undefined and what they together connote is in no way specified.

Once again, what is wrong with Euthyphro's statement is that it fails to define. By failing to articulate the characteristic trait of all unjust/punishable acts it gives us no idea of what all these acts have in common. And lacking a knowledge of their eidos or idea we still do not know how to identify a single instance of acts of this type. While formal enough logically, the definition fails to be "formal" in the Platonic sense and thus fails to give directions for its own practical use. And since it excludes nothing from the class of unjust/punishable acts it fails to insure the coherent application that Euthyphro would like to establish.

Mere verbal convention thus still leaves all questions of substance undecided, and leaves Euthyphro--lacking a knowledge of the form--still dependent on another type of convention--public opinion ungrounded in and unsupported by argument--as the sole basis of judgment. But public opinion, unguided by a clear idea of the essence of justice/holiness, is as we have seen inevitably inconsistent.

This is not a mere factual, possibly accidental inconsistency. For the reliance on literally uninformed--lacking knowledge of form--public opinion and tradition means a reliance on precedents, i.e. material examples unsupported by reasons as to why these precedents have ever been regarded as instances of justice/holiness. And it is not merely a fact that no particular act has always been regarded as just by all people at all times (a fact that fifth century investigators from Herodotus to the later Sophists were well aware of). Because of the relativity of material instances to their ever changing context no instance can ever be always an instance of whatever it may happen to instantiate in

63

this or that particular context. Therefore it is in principle impossible to find any particular act or thing universally just/holy. A mere enumeration of past precedents--even if correctly identified as instances, in their own context, of the thing in question--still leaves the class of universally just/approved-of/holy acts and things, those which are not and cannot ever be unjust/punishable/unholy undefined and possibly empty of content.

There is in fact something basically wrong and logically inadequate in all arguments supposedly based on precedents alone, and talking about precedent-use as radically opposed to the use of general rules and principles in judging particular cases is highly paradoxical. Though Socrates does not elaborate on this point here, it is clear that the challenge he sets for Euthyphro at the end of this section is one that Euthyphro is logically incapable of meeting. "Come now, Euthyphro...what is your proof that all the gods regard" your particular act right? (I.e. that when a murderous servant, bound by the master of the man he killed, dies while his master inquires into what ought to be done about him it is right for the son of the master to proceed against his father). "Come, try to show me clearly that all the gods certainly regard this act right." Euthyphro cannot answer the challenge, not merely because it is the case that there happens to be no precedent exactly like the situation in which Euthyphro finds himself, but because there can be no such precedent ever, in principle.

No two actual cases can ever be totally identical materially--involve the same persons doing the same act in the same way in the same historical, spatio-temporal context--and thus no case is in itself an exact "precedent" for any other case. The very use of precedents logically requires at least a minimum of abstraction from particular cases: a perception of partial identity, an identity in the relevant respect rather than in every respect. Thus it presupposes the user's ability to think in terms of more or less general ideas--common characteristics relevant, e.g. to justice/holiness--rather than merely in terms of particular cases.

Before Euthyphro, e.g. can use Zeus' chastising Cronus as a precedent for his prosecuting his father, he must perceive some relevant similarity between such dissimilar acts as Cronus devouring his children and Euthyphro's father contributing to a murderer's death by neglect. To classify both acts as cases of murder Euthyphro must have some general notion--however unclear, confused, or even wrong--of what constitutes wrongful homicide, at least in Greek custom or law, and find the two otherwise quite dissimilar cases similar, even identical in this respect, i.e. in their possession of the general mark or characteristic under which he subsumes both. Sheer precedent-use without any generalization

64

is a logically impossible operation. By its very nature precedent-use requires something other than precedent-use as its own basis: the employment of some however vague and unclarified notion on which the very selection of precedents qua precedents, i.e. relevantly similar cases, must be based. (In that, precedent-use is exactly like language use in any context--legal or other. Before we can point to anything as an instance of anything we must have a notion of what--general characteristic-- makes it an instance).

Every consideration so far has led us to the necessity of formal knowledge, knowledge of the eidos or idea, for the correct and reliable use of terms like holiness and justice, and it is not surprising that the remaining portion of Euthyphro Part I leads to the same conclusion. Through the preceding preliminary sections Socrates has laid an adequate foundation for his conclusive argument against Euthyphro and all public opinion based on mere traditional orthodoxy, and he can now proceed to deliver the final blow.

Notes

1. On this see Arnim, Platons Jugenddialoge p. 143.

2. Just as Polemarchus' uncritical acceptance of a perfectly correct definition of justice does not enable him to apply it correctly in Republic I.

3. Euthyphro adduces public acceptance, people's factual agreement rather than the logical impossibility of disagreement, as proof of its truth, while Socrates weakens even this acceptance to one of lip-service rather than actual agreement in thought, and accepts its expanded form "all gods and men agree that whoever is unjust must pay the penalty" only dialectically, as a starting point for a hypothetical argument rather than as something proven.

9C-11B Socrates:	But something occurred to me while you were talking, and I said to myself: Should Euthyphro prove to me ever so clearly that all the gods consider such a death unjust, what will I have learned from him about what is holy and unholy? For even if this act should seem to be hateful to the gods, we have just seen that what is and what is not holy cannot be defined this way because what was hateful to the gods appeared to be dear to them too. So I will not press you on this point, Euthyphro. Let all the gods regard this unjust and hateful if you wish; and we will amend our definition to state that whatever all the gods hate is unholy and what they all love is holy, and what some of them love and others hate is neither or both. Is this how you want us now to define what is holy and unholy?
Euthyphro:	Why not, Socrates?
So:	No reason, as far as I am concerned, Euthyphro; just consider if on this assumption you will find it easier to teach me what you promised.
Eu:	Well, then I will say that whatever all the gods love is holy, and the opposite, what all the gods hate, is unholy.
So:	Shall we now examine this statement too, Euthyphro, and ask if it is right, or shall we let it go and just accept what we and others say and agree that it is right merely because someone says so? Ought we not to inquire into what is stated here?
Eu:	We ought to, but I think the statement is now correct.
So:	We shall soon know about that my friend. But consider this: Is what is holy loved by the gods because it is holy, or is it holy·because it is loved by them?
Eu:	I do not understand what you mean, Socrates.
So:	I will try to explain. We speak of being carried and of carrying, being led and

leading, being seen and seeing. And you understand that in each of these cases there is a difference between the two terms and what the difference is.

Eu: I think I do.

So: And is not being loved likewise different from loving?

Eu: Yes, of course.

So: Tell me then, is what is carried "carried" because someone or something carries it or for some other reason?

Eu: For no other reason.

So: And what is led because someone or something leads it, and what is seen because someone or something sees it?

Eu: Yes.

So: Then it is not the case that one sees a thing because it is seen but, on the contrary, it is seen because one sees it; and one does not lead something because it is led but it is led because one leads it; and one does not carry something because it is carried but it is carried because one carries it? Is what I am trying to say clear to you, Euthyphro: That whenever anything becomes something or is affected in some way, it does not become because it is in a state of becoming but it is in a state of becoming because it becomes, and it is not affected because it is in a state of being affected but it is in a state of being affected because it is affected.

Eu: Right.

So: But is not that which is loved in a state of becoming or being affected?

Eu: Yes.

So: And is not this case analogous to the preceding ones: that whoever loves something

68

	does not love it because it is "loved" but it is "loved" because he loves it?
Eu:	Necessarily.
So:	Then what are we to say about what is holy, Euthyphro? That it is loved by all the gods, according to your definition?
Eu:	Yes.
So:	Because it is holy, or for some other reason?
Eu:	No, for that reason.
So:	It is loved because it is holy, and is not holy because it is loved?
Eu:	Quite.
So:	But what is loved by the gods and dear to them is loved and dear to them because it is loved?
Eu:	Of course.
So:	But then, that which is "god-loved" is not the same as that which is holy, Euthyphro, nor what is holy the same as what is god-loved, but the two are different, according to what you say.
Eu:	How so, Socrates?
So:	Because we have agreed that what is holy is loved because it is holy and is not holy because it is loved, have we not?
Eu:	Yes, we have.
So:	And what is god-loved is god-loved because the gods love it rather than that they love it because it is god-loved?
Eu:	True.
So:	But my dear Euthyphro, if what is god-loved and what is holy were the same, then if what is holy is loved because it is holy, what is god-loved would be loved by the gods because

69

it is god-loved; conversely, if what is god-loved is god-loved because it is loved by the gods, then what is holy would be holy because it is loved by them; but now you see that the opposite is the case and the two things are altogether different from each other. For the one is loved because someone loves it while the other is loved because it is in itself lovable.[1] And so, Euthyphro, it seems that when you were asked about what is holy you were unwilling to reveal to me its essential nature; instead you told me something incidental, something that happens to what is holy, namely that it is loved by all the gods. But what it really is you have not told me.

Although Euthyphro does not take up Socrates' challenge to show that all the gods agree in holding his act right—quite wisely, since his approach to the problem makes it impossible for him to meet the challenge—Socrates now focusses on further difficulties with Euthyphro's definition which go to the very heart of the problem.

Even assuming that Euthyphro or anyone else could prove that there are actions loved by all and hated by none of the gods, and amended the definition from "what is holy is what is god-loved" to "what is holy is what is loved by all the gods and hated by none", this amended definition still would not reveal the nature of holiness in such a way that whoever knows the definition can use it as a paradigm for determining by and for himself what is holy in every situation where he might have to make such determination.

After his customary warning against accepting the new definition "merely because someone says it is correct" (9E) Socrates proceeds to testing its paradigmatic worth by asking: "Is what is holy loved by the gods because it is holy, or is it holy because it is loved by the gods?"

The "because" (dia ti, dia touto hoti, dioti) in the previous question is ambiguous; it may signify a logical, existential, causal, or teleological connection between the clauses it connects, and Socrates' use of it in the course of this section manages to convey all these senses. Since Euthyphro does not understand the question when it is first raised Socrates proceeds to explain.

What is "loved", "carried", "led" or "seen" is obviously "loved", "carried", "led" or "seen" because someone in fact loves,

70

carries, leads or sees it. It is the act of an agent (loving, etc.) that makes the thing what it is (loved, etc.), puts it into a certain state of being, rather than the other way around. Were the act not performed by any agent the thing would not have the characteristic (being loved, etc.) that it acquires solely by virtue of the act being performed. The performance of the act (loving) is the necessary precondition for and the sole cause of the state of being (being loved) of the thing. The thing undergoes a change, becomes something, acquires a property (being loved) because of the act; and the act is not done, does not come into being, because or for the reason that the thing is antecedently in that state or has that property.

So the question Socrates is asking is which of the two characteristics involved in Euthyphro's definition, "holy" and "godloved", is prior to the other in the sense of being the antecedent condition for a consequent one, the cause of an effect, the reason for the other coming into being or becoming predicable of the thing. Is it the gods' loving something that makes a thing holy, or is it the holiness of the thing that makes the gods love it?

This question is not sprung on Euthyphro out of nowhere. Socrates' insistence all through the preceding sections of the dialogue on objective standards, paradigmatic ideas as prerequisites for informed judgment, affirmed the priority of such standards and of an insight into them as a precondition for making correct judgments about particular cases. And trying to show clearly that his own action was dear to, loved by the gods—and therefore holy—Euthyphro agreed with the stipulation that "whatever (the gods) consider fair and good and just they love, and the opposite of these things they hate" (7E). This stipulation states that there is a precondition for the gods' act of loving: it is their considering something fair and good and just that makes them love the thing. The things they love are of themselves fair and good and just antecedently to their act of loving. It is precisely this state of being (fair and good and just) that makes them in themselves lovable (hoion phileisthai 11A), worthy of love, and induces, motivates, determines the gods' loving them. This alone is what makes the gods' love rational rather than totally willful and arbitrary, that they have a reason for doing what they do instead of doing something (loving particular things) for no reason at all.

Understood in this light, in the context of the entire course of the dialogue so far, Socrates' question "Is what is holy loved by the gods because it is holy or holy because it is loved?" is momentous. What he is asking is, in fact, whether "holiness" is a characteristic or state of being wholly independent of the gods' acts (of loving or not loving), and is thus a property of acts or things capable of independent determination (i.e. independent of

ascertaining what the gods do or do not love). If "holiness"
functions like "being lovable, worthy of love" rather than like
"being loved" in the preceding examples, then "holy" and "god-
loved", the terms involved in Euthyphro's definition, are as different as "lovable i.e. worthy of love" and "loved"; the latter
("loved") designation being dependent on someone's act (of loving), the former not only independent of the act but the precondition, cause, reason for the act being correctly performed. (And
even the incorrect performance of the act, i.e. loving something
that is not really lovable, is necessarily preceded and motivated
by a mistaken judgment about the thing's lovability. It is an
ignorant but not irrational act).

Whether or not Euthyphro fully understands all the ramifica-
tions of the question his answer is that the priority among these
terms is what one would have judged it to be in the light of the
previous discussion: What is holy is loved because it is holy
and for this reason, and not holy because it is loved.

Once Euthyphro makes this admission Socrates' case is dialectically complete. If what is holy is loved by the gods because it is holy while what is god-loved is god-loved (theophiles)
because they happen to love it, then the two terms—"holy" and
"god-loved"—are as different as lovable and loved, useful and
used, edible and eaten. The class of things holy and the class
of things god-loved are not necessarily the same in extension,
and the manner in which one determines what falls into the first
class is quite different from the way one determines what falls
into the second.

Since now "holy" is analogous to "lovable" or "worthy of being loved" rather than to "loved"—i.e. whatever happens to be
loved for whatever reason, right or wrong, or even for no reason
at all if that should be conceivable—"god-loved" fails to define
"holy", and Euthyphro's definition "whatever all the gods love is
holy" breaks down. "God-loved" is, at best, merely a pathos of
what is holy, i.e. something that happens to it because it is
what it is (holy). It is a consequent characteristic rather than
an essential one (ousia). Even if it were a necessary consequent
given certain conditions, e.g. if whatever the gods happened to
perceive to be holy they necessarily loved,[2] that would still fail
to make it a necessary consequent in every case.

For it has not been stipulated that the gods know what is
holy—know the universal mark, the eidos or idea common to all
instances of holiness—and thus necessarily recognize, and therefore love, holiness in all its instances. Thus there might be
holy things that the gods fail to recognize and therefore fail to
love. Nor has it been stipulated or proved that the gods have
experienced all possible instances of holiness, and so there might

72

be holy things no god ever came across and therefore no god in fact happened to love. Thus the class of holy things might in fact be much larger than the class of (actually) god-loved things. Furthermore, it has not been stipulated or proved that the gods love nothing but what is holy[3] and so, even if they necessarily loved all that is holy, the class of god-loved (theophiles) things might be greater than the class of things holy.

The upshot of all this is that as long as holiness is logically separable from and definable independently of the gods' love, being god-loved is not an essential characteristic of all holy things and acts, and holiness cannot be defined in terms of the gods' loving or not loving whatever they may or may not love.

Now if we accept the validity of the argument, given the assumptions Euthyphro makes or concedes, the question remains what exactly has the argument accomplished in the context of the portion of the dialogue we have dealt with so far? Has it really delivered a crippling blow to Euthyphro's last attempt by demonstrating the impossibility of defining holiness as what is loved by (all) the gods? And has it provided, or at least given a clue for finding, a tenable substantive definition of holiness? We shall discuss these questions in turn.

Although the possibility that Socrates' argument is invalid and that Socrates knows this cannot be ruled out a priori, I see no reason for not conceding the logical validity of the argument. This leaves open the question whether the premises of the argument themselves can be shown to be necessary in the context of the previous portions of the dialogue, or if they are no more than mere hypotheses, stipulated but not argued for, so that the conclusion of the argument itself remains hypothetical rather than necessary.

A number of interpreters[4] take the latter view. They admit the strict validity of Socrates' argument, but regard the argument itself as merely dialectical rather than philosophically conclusive. Euthyphro, they assert, is checkmated by the argument merely because he agreed to certain premises which were incompatible with the definition he proposed. But since there was no need for Euthyphro to accept the premises in question in the first place, he could still reject the conclusion and stick to his definition by simply rejecting the premises he so foolishly accepted. And that is, it is asserted, what a philosophically sophisticated interlocutor would have done in Euthyphro's case.

The crucial premise in question is, of course, that what is holy is loved (by the gods) because it is holy rather than holy because it is loved (10D). This is the premise that religious voluntarists of a certain type would reject so as to be able to

define what is holy, or absolutely good, in a Euthyphronean manner
(as what is loved, willed, commanded, etc. by God or the gods).
Kierkegaard, e.g. is clearly a defender of this position in that
he emphatically rejects the proposition that what is holy or absolutely good or ultimately essential for man is definable independently of God's (from the human point of view irrational and
incomprehensible) will or command. Now is there something in the
dialogue to prevent Euthyphro from taking a thoroughly Kierkegaardian stance? Are there premises, explicit or implied, which
Euthyphro has accepted that make his rejection of this premise
logically impossible?

I think there are two basic presuppositions in the Euthyphro
that do just that, and only dealing with the argument (10C-11B)
out of context, as if it stood by itself rather than followed and
built upon the previous discussion, makes it possible for the
reader to regard the Kierkegaardian alternative as open for
Euthyphro to adopt. These two presuppositions are: A) that holiness is knowable, and B) that holiness is a virtue.

A) All through the dialogue Euthyphro claims to know and be
able to teach Socrates—who claims not to know—what is holy. It
is these claims that are the starting point of the Socratic elenctic, and the entire inquiry conducted focusses on knowledge: Does
Euthyphro know, and can he help Socrates to know, what is holy?
(Indeed, this claim underlies, as we have seen, Meletus' indictment of Socrates as well as the city's institution of impiety
trials; that is what makes Euthyphro a true representative of the
city itself).

And "knowledge" has not been left undefined. We have seen
that knowledge is knowledge of forms. What the knower knows is
the eidos or idea; not just instances but the one single universal mark or characteristic that is common to all instances of the
quality or thing he claims to know.

So far "what is loved by all the gods" might satisfy the requirements of knowledge. The definition is clearly universal.
If what is holy is simply what is loved by all the gods then "being loved by all the gods" is a universal mark or characteristic
that all holy things necessarily share, and might thus qualify as
expressive of the form of all that is holy.

But there is a further qualification of knowledge that
Euthyphro's definition is incapable of satisfying, and that is its
practical, paradigmatic character. In the Euthyphro Socrates is
asking for a definition (of the form) of holiness that he can use
as a practical paradigm, i.e. as a guide for determining, on his
own and by his own unaided effort, what is holy and what is unholy
in each and every conceivable situation. It is only having such a

paradigm that would make him a knower: someone who does not have to rely on what anyone else--man or god--says on the subject, does not have to depend on others' instruction or command in each individual case, but can decide the matter himself, and having done so can argue his case and test others' judgments by investigating whether they accord with or contradict the essential nature of holiness as specified by the definition (6E). To have knowledge, as distinguished from mere opinion, means to be autonomous in judgment while the possession of mere opinions implies heteronomy: a dependence on something other than one's own rational thought for determining one's beliefs, attitudes and action.

Now it is clear that Euthyphro's definition "what is holy is what is loved by all the gods", interpreted in the manner of the suggested alternative (what is holy is not loved because it is holy but is holy because it is loved), provides no standard capable of paradigmatic use. For how could one ever know--and thus be able to use as a criterion for determining what is holy in each case--what the gods happen to love and hate? Since we no longer have a definition of holiness independent of the gods' love, and the gods love what they love without reason--for the objects of their love have no common, objective characteristic which makes them the necessary objects of divine love--how could anyone ever know what may or may not be the object of the gods' now wholly arbitrary and irrational love? In the absence of an independent definition of what is "lovable to", i.e. "worthy of being loved by", the gods, the specification "god-loved" (theophiles) would not necessarily include or exclude any particular act or thing in or from the class of god-loved things. Instead of defining i.e. literally drawing boundaries around all that is holy, it would merely substitute one unknown and in fact unknowable term (god-loved) for another (holy) and thus add nothing to our knowledge of holiness--or more correctly, it would not alleviate our ignorance of holiness by one iota.

It would not help at all to claim that since everyone is brought up within the city's religious tradition everyone already "knows" what the gods love and hate. For even if we stipulated that the founders and transmitters of that tradition could have conceivably known what the gods loved, they could not possibly transmit their "knowledge" to anyone else. For now that all god-loved things and acts no longer have a common characteristic besides being god-loved, all that could be transmitted by tradition are particular examples of what the gods, at one time or another, happened to love, rather than the universal idea which would enable the receivers of the tradition themselves to identify all instances of what is god-loved now or ever, in all conceivable situations. Thus even if the poets' stories happened to be true, those who relied on them would have only (particular) opinions about rather than a knowledge (of the universal form) of what is god-loved.

75

And of course the stipulation of the truth of the traditional stories is one that Socrates is not only unwilling to make, as we have seen, but simply cannot make in terms of his definition of knowledge. Not because tradition may be uninformed, and therefore mistaken, but because--in terms of the alternative now proposed--it is necessarily uninformed. If what is god-loved is incapable of being defined in terms of a universal mark or characteristic that all god-loved things have in common--and this is exactly what the alternative proposed implies--tradition, public opinion, and all men at all times are necessarily ignorant of what is god-loved since there is in fact nothing one could conceivably know here about what the gods may or may not love. No one can therefore stipulate the truth of tradition except arbitrarily. In the absence of a knowable criterion of truth of what the poets say about the gods' love the question of the truth of tradition cannot even be raised meaningfully.

Even if, in spite of these considerations, someone chose to accept the truth of tradition and believe that the poets correctly identified what was god-loved in the particular cases they dealt with, still one would be left utterly without knowledge of what is holy/god-loved and therefore without any guidance for making a single decision about holiness even in cases resembling those the poets happened to present.[5] For on the alternative theory (that what is holy is holy because god-loved and not v. v.) there is no guarantee whatsoever that what the gods, or even a single god, ever happened to love in any particular case would ever again be loved by them, or him, in any other situation at any other time. Now that the gods' love has become utterly irrational and arbitrary, since they have no reason for loving or hating anything whatever, even the gods could not conceivably know what they might happen to love at any moment in the future, and thus even divine inspiration on the part of the poets, or immediate revelation to a single individual by a single god appearing in awesome majesty, would fail to provide men with a usable paradigm of what is holy/god-loved at all times. As long as the gods themselves are not <u>bound</u> to love something <u>because</u> <u>it</u> <u>has</u> <u>certain</u> <u>characteristics</u> <u>prior</u> <u>to</u> <u>and</u> <u>independent</u> <u>of</u> <u>their</u> <u>loving</u> <u>it</u> every act (of loving) of theirs is an utterly unique act giving no indication whatsoever of how they might act at any other time. The type of consistency that Euthyphro himself insisted on in criticizing others' judgment of his case (6A), as well as the consistency Euthyphro and Socrates together regarded a sine qua non of a tenable definition and used as a reason for rejecting Euthyphro's second proposal (6E-8B), can no longer be required and insisted upon in matters involving holiness and divine love. Consistency is a rational criterion which must be given up where rationality itself--the gods having a <u>reason</u> for loving something-- is set aside. And with consistency and rationality abandoned the very notion of knowledge--theoretical or practical--and knowability fall by the wayside.

This is exactly Kierkegaard's point. Unlike the interpreters
who cite his position as an alternative to the one Euthyphro "so
foolishly" accepts, Kierkegaard saw quite clearly the logical
consequences of taking the alternative point of view: It makes a
knowledge of what is holy, or good, or loved, or commanded by
(the gods or) God utterly impossible. It leaves the man of faith
utterly without guidance and in the throes of fear and trembling.
It takes away all human autonomy and makes men completely dependent on God's (or the gods') unique and inscrutable commands. In
other words it violates every Socratic stricture concerning paradigmatic knowledge and is thus totally irresponsive to the central
Socratic demand in the dialogue (as well as being irreconcilable
with Euthyphro's or the Athenian public's claim to know. Since
on a semi-Kierkegaardian position no one could ever tell who may
or may not be doing what is god-loved or commanded, no one could
indict anyone for impiety, and Meletus, Euthyphro's, and the
city's court-cases would collapse).

B) Before we raise the question whether this demand itself
could be abandoned, and the alternative definition saved simply
by abandoning Euthyphro's claim to knowledge, we have to consider
another claim that functions as the starting point and presupposition of the inquiry here: the claim that holiness or piety is a
virtue, i.e. something whose possession improves, makes excellent,
whatever possesses it--be it individual, family or state.

We have seen[6] that in fifth century popular religious-moral
thought holiness was a virtue often so closely associated with
justice, and indeed every other virtue, as to be practically synonymous with virtue as such. At least the first part of this
attitude is certainly shared by the interlocutors in the Euthyphro.
Holiness or piety is regarded to be a virtue by all the direct and
indirect participants in the dialogue.

The occasion for the dialogue, and the point of departure
for the entire discussion, is Meletus' charge which specifies
that Socrates' impious activity corrupts, lessens the excellence
of, the youth and thereby the state itself, and it is this corruption that justifies Meletus' and the city's prosecution of Socrates. Socrates' lack of a virtue--piety--is alleged to lessen the
virtue--excellence, well-functioning--of his associates and, ultimately, of the city itself.

Euthyphro regards unholiness no less a vice--a pathological
condition that undermines the health of the organism in which it
exists--than do Meletus and the city. Right at the start he justifies his proceeding against his father by claiming that the latter's unholy act has polluted and endangered the very existence

of his family. And increasingly Euthyphro associates holiness
and justice, in the end defending his definition of holiness as
what is loved by all the gods by no other proof than that all the
gods necessarily hate injustice, i.e. the lack of (a particular)
virtue. Were Euthyphro to abandon his view that piety is a virtue, his whole position, in the court and in the dialogue, would
lose whatever justification it has in Euthyphro's eyes.

Socrates, for his part, has no argument with Meletus' and
Euthyphro's claim that unholiness corrupts and is therefore a
vice. He agrees that impious acts such as he is alleged to have
committed--teaching others wrong ideas about what is holy, i.e.
truly awesome, venerable and good, and what is unholy, i.e. awful,
detestable and abhorrent--do indeed corrupt the people involved
and make them, and ultimately the city itself, less excellent.
What he claims is not that impiety does not corrupt and destroy,
and piety does not safeguard and heal, but merely that Meletus
and Euthyphro, and the city itself, do not know what is truly
pious and impious. There is simply nothing in the dialogue as
far as we have read that would indicate a less than total agree-
ment--between Socrates, Euthyphro, Meletus and the city--on this
point that holiness or piety is indeed a virtue.

But given this basic presupposition, agreed upon by all the
participants, direct or indirect, it is immediately evident that
Euthyphro is in no position to defend his definition by adopting
the suggested alternative that what is holy is holy merely because
it is loved by the gods, and that therefore holiness cannot be
defined independently of the gods' act of loving what they happen
to love.

If piety is a virtue--something that necessarily improves,
makes excellent, the life of whatever possesses it--then all pious
acts do have a common characteristic other than being merely god-
loved, and this characteristic is not only specifiable and knowable without reference to the gods' love but even restricts its
range by setting limits to what the gods themselves may love and
hate. (E.g. unlike Kierkegaard's God, Euthyphro's gods cannot
condone let alone command murder). Even if the gods should
necessarily love what is virtuous—the source of improvement rather than corruption to individual and society--and hate what is
vicious, the designation of piety as a virtue makes it impossible
for Euthyphro not to agree with what he in fact assents to in the
dialogue that the gods love whatever they love because it is holy
(virtuous) rather than that it is holy (virtuous) because they
love it. Piety being a virtue sets up a demand to which the gods
themselves must conform rather than leaving the matter of holiness
to their arbitrary decision--to love and thus hallow whatever they
please. (Contrary to Kierkegaard's position in Sickness Unto
Death, the opposite of vice here is virtue and not irrational

faith and an absolute reliance on the totally inscrutable and arbitrary will of the gods).

The very charge Meletus makes against Socrates on behalf of
the city implies that Meletus and the city share Euthyphro's
attitude--that the gods must love what they love because it has
some characteristic specifiable independently of their love it-
self--even to the point of judging what can and what cannot qualify as a true god, i.e. a god the city can and must recognize.
For he accuses Socrates of introducing new, and somehow false,
unholy deities; deities who in some unspecified manner fail to
contribute to and safeguard the city's welfare. What he condemns
here is in fact what seems to him Kierkegaardian in Socrates'
position: that he follows his own private, communally unknown
and possibly unknowable daimon's commands, disregarding the dele-
terious effects of this type of behavior on the community's welfare. (At least that is how Euthyphro interprets Meletus' "intro-
duction of new deities" charge).

Meletus' and Euthyphro's situation here is much the same as
that of Thrasymachus in Republic I, where Thrasymachus is, by virtue of the concessions he has made, as incapable of adopting
Cleitophon's suggestion concerning his definition of justice as
Euthyphro is of adopting the alternative suggested by the interpreters here. For having insisted on justice being a virtue, i.e.
something that is beneficial to the possessor himself, Thrasymachus can no longer define what is just simply as "what the ruler
or ruling party commands". Though even in Cleitophon's suggestion
the ruler's will is not as irrational and arbitrary as that of the
Kierkegaardian God,7 given the possible ignorance of the rulers
about what will actually benefit them their commanding something
cannot by itself make it just (the way Cleitophon's definition
would have it). Justice, being a virtue, necessarily has an independent (from the ruler's will) definition, and all just acts
necessarily share a common characteristic ("beneficial to the
possessor") which is specifiable without reference to the ruler's
will or command. That is why Thrasymachus is not only unable to
accept Cleitophon's suggestion; he has to insist on knowledge
even to the extent of redefining the term "ruler" to mean, in the
strict sense, only someone who knows, and therefore necessarily
commands, what is to his own advantage. (A stipulation not altogether unlike Meletus' about what kind of gods the city can
recognize as gods).

We shall return later (in the Postscript) to this analogy
between the problems Euthyphro and Thrasymachus encounter in defining holiness and justice, and elaborate on it further in order
to show the applicability of the Euthyphro's arguments concerning
holiness to all philosophical inquiry into the nature and function
of justice. But there is an additional point that is important to

make here concerning the relation of the two presuppositions we consider basic to the entire enquiry in the Euthyphro.

If holiness is a virtue, i.e. something that necessarily improves its possessor's life, then all things holy share a common characteristic, an eidos or idea which is knowable (without reference to the gods' scrutable or inscrutable love) and, unlike the alternative suggested for Euthyphro's adoption, usable as a practical paradigm in the Socratic sense.

At the same time if what is holy (and virtuous) is knowable, our knowledge itself of what is holy (as such and in the particular context) becomes the necessary and sufficient condition of our having this virtue, i.e. amounts to its possession. Since every man who knows what is good necessarily does what is good as a practically rational, teleological being, whoever knows what is holy (wholesome, improving, most beneficial) necessarily acts in accordance with this knowledge and is therefore eo ipso characterized by holiness; his knowledge by itself generates and guarantees holy behavior. This in turn makes a knowledge of holiness supremely important to every man. Because it is not some kind of abstract, theoretical, and practically irrelevant knowledge which one may or may not want to have but a knowledge of what contributes to the excellent life, every man by nature—qua rational, teleological—necessarily desires and pursues this knowledge provided he is aware of not yet having it.

This is, after all, what justifies the Euthyphro's inquiry as such. Since holiness is a virtue, its knowledge, that toward which the entire inquiry is directed here, is a most important type of knowledge, a knowledge of immense moral significance. And since whoever is aware of not possessing this knowledge will necessarily strive for it if he believes holiness to be a virtue, the Socratic testing of Euthyphro's knowledge, designed to reveal Euthyphro's ignorance of the subject in question, should contribute to Euthyphro's striving for and acquiring the knowledge (and the virtue) he does not yet have. It is not an abstract inquiry but a process of moral education, an exhibition of Socrates not corrupting but trying to improve his interlocutors, and thus an indirect refutation of Meletus' charge.

That Euthyphro may in fact be unimprovable because, as we shall see, he does not possess enough intelligence to become fully aware of his ignorance does not weaken Socrates' argument or defense. It merely constitutes an indictment of Euthyphro, and by extension of Meletus and the Athenian public, who notwithstanding their well-nigh incorrigible ignorance claim to know and to be entitled to judge matters they know nothing about. Though they are of course incapable of understanding Socrates' point, the philosophical reader at whom the dialogue is directed ought not to be.

Now given these interdependent and mutually reinforcing presuppositions it is obvious that Euthyphro, or at least the thoughtful reader, cannot adopt a quasi-Kierkegaardian alternative, and thus Socrates' argument here (9C-11B) is far from being as hypothetical and merely dialectical as it appears to be when taken out of context. Given its presuppositions it is a complete and conclusive philosophical argument. Its seeming lack of force, the lack so many interpreters point to, is solely the result of the interpreters ignoring precisely those presuppositions which make the conclusion of the argument necessary in the context of the dialogue.

One might, I suppose, still question the philosophical necessity of these presuppositions themselves, and ask if Euthyphro might not escape the conclusion they lead to simply by rejecting them so as to be able to adopt the alternative position.

After all, this is precisely what Kierkegaard does, up to a point; indeed, this is the position Kierkegaard occasionally attributes to Socrates himself. Taking the Socratic profession of ignorance (about holiness and, in general, virtue) literally, he points to Socrates invoking his daimon as evidence of Socrates' own reliance on unique and inscrutable divine commands for the direction of his particular acts. Which is, of course, what Socrates would in fact have to rely on given the absence of knowable paradigmatic ethical rules and the total impossibility of all moral knowledge.

But this is a rather desperate solution to Euthyphro's problems. Even if one attributed to Socrates himself a kind of Kierkegaardian teleological suspension of the ethical and the consequent relinquishing of man's rational autonomy and total dependence on an irrational faith in equally irrational gods—an attitude which even Kierkegaard admits was utterly alien to the Greeks—it is clear that neither Euthyphro nor Meletus or the Athenian public could adopt this alternative without completely vitiating their position and depriving their own action—prosecuting those they consider guilty of impiety—of all justification.

For their entire case rests on the double claim that they know what is pious and impious, and that piety is a virtue and impiety a vice which, since it threatens the well-being of the community, the community has the right and even the obligation to guard against by taking whatever action might be proper for its prevention and cure. Giving up these claims they would have to give up prosecuting Socrates or anyone else for impiety. For the possibility that those who seem to them impious might well be, like Kierkegaard's Abraham, divinely inspired "holy criminals"

81

whose madness is far superior to any merely human sanity, would be wide open.

Whether or not they could even then proceed to an outright Kierkegaardian position and assert that madness, or at least a certain type of madness, not only might be but necessarily is a sign of a more than human sanity is doubtful. But that is a question we hardly need to consider in the context of Euthyphro's and Meletus' actions as presented in the dialogue.

As to Socrates himself, his situation is at least superficially different with regard to these claims in that, unlike Euthyphro or Meletus, he does not make them in the dialogue. He neither claims to know what is holy, nor is he prosecuting anyone for unholiness; nor does he in the Euthyphro itself even claim to be innocent of the charges and to be a healer rather than a corruptor of the state. (He does make these claims in the Apology, but in the Euthyphro it is Euthyphro, not Socrates, who asserts Socrates' innocence and Meletus' guilt in so many words. 3A).

So in terms of what is explicitly asserted by Socrates himself in the dialogue, it might not be inconsistent for Socrates to doubt that piety, whatever it might be, is a virtue, and that piety, for all his opponents' claim to knowledge, is in fact knowable. Certainly the argument of Euthyphro 9E-11C is sufficient to prove only that if piety is a virtue it cannot be defined as Euthyphro seeks to define it whichever of the alternatives proposed—pious because god-loved or god-love because pious—one might wish to adopt. Likewise the argument proves that if piety were defined as "what is god-loved, because it is god-loved" it would be unknowable, and on the alternative definition—god-loved because pious—it would still remain undefined and unknown. But that piety is in fact a virtue and that it is knowable the argument itself does not prove, as the interpreters who propose the alternative interpretation quite rightly point out. (Even the fact that so far Euthyphro has been unable to define piety shows merely that he is ignorant; but such ignorance might be the necessary consequence of piety being an unknowable and therefore undefinable quality.)

Nevertheless Socrates' position concerning the status of piety—as a virtue and as knowable—is not significantly different from Meletus' and Euthyphro's. He does share these basic presuppositions with his opponents; they are in fact the common presuppositions from which the entire argument of the Euthyphro proceeds and without which neither this dialogue nor Socrates' lifelong philosophical activity would make sense.

At the very beginning of the dialogue Socrates wholeheartedly agrees with Meletus' position that impiety interpreted as a corruption of the youth, or indeed anyone else, is a vice deserving the utmost attention on the part of the city and its citizens whose well-being it truly threatens. And nowhere in the dialogue does he take issue with Euthyphro's argument that impiety, being a kind of pollution, must be extirpated and whatever it has polluted must be purified no matter who committed the act. The only issue Socrates has with Meletus and Euthyphro is not whether piety, rightly conceived, is a virtue but whether Meletus and Euthyphro know what this virtue truly consists in.

There is not the slightest indication anywhere in the Euthyphro or its companion dialogues[8] that Socrates regards holiness to be anything but virtuous. That there is such a thing as holiness, i.e. that there are things in the world which are truly awesome and venerable, holy in the sense of being by nature wholesome, necessarily contributory to human well-being and thus a prerequisite for the excellent life, Socrates never doubts. Nor does he doubt that there are acts and things unholy, i.e. truly awful, by nature corruptive and destructive of human well-being, and thus necessarily abhorrent and destestable. For to deny this would mean to deny the very existence of virtue as such and not merely that of holiness or piety as a virtue. Virtue is human excellence: that by virtue of which a man's life is improved and made as good as possible, and vice is the opposite of this. On the presupposition that nothing holy and unholy, wholesome and destructive, greatly beneficial and greivously harmful, i.e. simply good and evil to men, exists in the world, virtue itself would be inconceivable, and so would be, in the end, all rational teleological behavior on the part of men. For such behavior, teleological, aim-directed activity as such, is necessarily directed at what the agent considers to be good rather than evil for him, and the total absence of things holy and unholy would be equivalent to the total absence of anything good or evil, a total absence of anything that could provide rational direction for action.

Therefore Socrates' life-long concern for and inquiry into virtue, the concern he manifests and the inquiry he engages in in the Euthyphro no less than in any of the other early dialogues, is logically incompatible with his denying that holiness is a very real and meaningful notion and that our notions about what things and acts are truly holy—wholesome, healing, beneficial, good—do play an all-important role in human action and life.

By the same token it would be incompatible with Socrates' life-long activity, including his activity in the Euthyphro, to hold that what is and what is not holy is unknowable. For once again the unknowability of what is holy—in the end what is truly good and evil in human life--would make all inquiry into holiness, and indeed into virtue as such, senseless.

It would be no good saying that the purpose of the inquiry might be precisely to establish the fact that holiness is indeed unknowable. In the first place the dialogue argues and establishes no such thing; that Euthyphro and Meletus are ignorant of what piety is does not prove this virtue's unknowability. In the second place, trying to establish the unknowability of piety would be a rather self-contradictory enterprise. For if holiness were indeed unknowable then no one could conceivably know what holiness is in any respect whatsoever, and that means no one could conceivably know or attempt to prove that it is unknowable. This is what Socrates points out at the end of the Meno after he has led Meno to the quasi-Euthyphronian view that virtue is the result of divine dispensation which men receive without understanding (Meno 100A-B). Of course Socrates might still believe, even if not know, that virtue is not a matter of knowledge, but if he did that the inquiry in the Meno as well as in the Euthyphro would become senseless, for Socrates could no longer hold "that believing that we ought to inquire into what we do not know will make us better and manlier and less helpless than we would be if we held that it is impossible to find out and unnecessary to search for what we do not know" (86B-C), and he could no longer be "determined to fight for this belief by word and deed" as he indeed does both in the Meno and the Euthyphro. On the presupposition of the unknowability of virtue or holiness, the right approach to the Euthyphro's, or the Meno's, subject would be not philosophical inquiry but prayer; an asking for divine inspiration that is itself justified by nothing but a rationally unjustified faith. But that is obviously not what takes place in the Euthyphro or any other Socratic dialogue. That virtue as such, or at least holiness, the virtue that is the subject of the Euthyphro, is a matter of irrational faith requiring the total relinquishing of human autonomy and a total submission to the inscrutable love, will or command of irrational gods is precisely the position Socrates opposes with every argument in his power in the Euthyphro.

It is time now to raise the much debated question concerning the positive conclusions, if any, of the Socratic inquiry as far as it has progressed by the end of Euthyphro Part I. Given the basic presuppositions--that piety is a virtue and that piety is knowable--which Socrates and his opponents share, Socrates' argument against Euthyphro's definitions seems to be inescapable. But where does that leave us? Has Socrates succeeded merely in demolishing Euthyphro's definitions, or has he also provided, or at least provided the clues for finding, an acceptable definition of his own? Is Part I of the Euthyphro merely negative, or does it contain positive and substantive conclusions which follow from even though they are not made explicit by the Socratic argument? The answer to this question is, I think, implicit in the preceding discussion.

84

Given the presuppositions on which alone the inquiry Socrates
undertakes in the Euthyphro--or any other early dialogue--makes
sense, the Socratic definition of piety must be the same as that
of any other virtue, indeed as that of virtue as such. Piety or
holiness, the right reverence for what is truly venerable and
proper fear of what is truly fearful, consists in nothing other
than the knowledge of what is truly awesome and awful, wholesome
and destructive, i.e. simply good and evil in human life. This
knowledge being for Socrates the necessary and sufficient condition of human excellence as such, its possession is tantamount to
the possession of this, or any other, virtue.

Of course, piety or holiness so defined can no longer be
separated from any other part of virtue, indeed from virtue as
such, but that is hardly surprising seeing that no other part or
aspect of virtue--courage, temperance, justice, etc.--is any more
separable from the whole of virtue in the early dialogues than
this one turns out to be in the Euthyphro. Virtue, in all these
dialogues, is one; it is wisdom, the knowledge of human good and
evil, and there are no truly independent virtues, here or anywhere
else, to be found in the Socratic dialogues.

What gives piety nevertheless a somewhat special status among
the virtues Socrates is wont to discuss, and this is what may account for the relative neglect of this virtue in the dialogues
subsequent to the Euthyphro, is that unlike the other virtues
which can at least be focussed on individually because they may
be said to have a special domain of application, piety cannot be
singled out and focussed upon in this manner. For courage, which
as the knowledge of what to fear and what to dare is just about
literally eusebeia, is virtue (knowledge of good and evil) exercised in situations of great personal danger. And temperance--
sane, wholesome, saving thought--is the same virtue (self-knowledge, the knowledge of what is and what is not good for one) with
special reference to its exercise in the conduct of the individual's daily life, while justice might be specified as the exercise
of the same thing (knowledge of one's own natural function and
good) in the individual's relation to others. Although even these
distinctions are rather hard to maintain, and Socrates does not
consistently maintain them in the early dialogues, it is not only
difficult but just about impossible to maintain a similar distinction with respect to piety by assigning a special domain of operation to this virtue.

For the only obvious answer to the question what this special
domain might be is that the exercise of this particular virtue
pertains to men's relationship to and dealings with the gods rather than his fellow men. But we have seen that this distinction,
although traditionally made, is not in fact a real distinction in
the traditional view. In fifth century popular religion piety or

holiness was not conspicuously restricted to matters involving
men's immediate relationship to the gods. Just about every aspect of human wrongdoing, whether or not it involved such direct
relations, could be and was at one time or other considered impious. Since the gods qua guardians of the city were intimately
though possibly indirectly involved in every important sphere and
aspect of social and individual life, this could hardly be otherwise. The notion of the unity of virtues was implicit in traditional Greek thought concerning holiness or piety long before
Plato made it explicit in the early and middle dialogues.

And the argument of Part I of the Euthyphro leads to precisely the same conclusion. Euthyphro, too, starts in the traditional
manner trying to define piety with reference to some or even all
the gods. But by the time Socrates concludes his questioning
just before the central break in the dialogue, the argument has
established that it is at best superfluous and uninformative and
at worst impossible to bring in the gods in an attempt to define
the nature and domain of piety. For if the gods love what is holy
because it is holy—now, in the widest sense of the word, simply
good, right, just, fair, wholesome, in human life—then even if
it were shown that the gods necessarily loved all these things
they would then love all that is good rather than merely some
special part of it that might concern men's immediate relationship
to them. And in order to know what is holy one would have to know
what is good independently of and without any reference to the
gods' love. Therefore one could simply forget about the gods in
attempting to define what is holy. Nor is any reference to them
needed even when it comes to sanctioning this virtue. For if
what is holy is what is good, wholesome, beneficial to man, then
quite apart from the gods' happening or not happening to love
holiness and hate impiety every individual already has the strongest possible motivation for doing what is holy, i.e. good. As a
teleological being he cannot rationally aim at anything other than
what he considers good. And so, if he only knows what is holy he
will necessarily do what is holy even without the gods presumably
sanctioning such behavior.

If on the other hand we adopt the alternative proposal, that
what is holy is holy merely because the gods love it, and therefore holiness has no independent (of the gods' love) definition,
then, as the argument has shown, no reference to the gods and
their arbitrary and irrational love can possibly define holiness
and provide man with a practical paradigm he can ever use in determining, and conforming to, what is holy. If so, holiness not
only does not have a special domain of application, as in the
former case, but as a totally undefined concept it has no knowable
domain of application whatever. Thus the reference to the gods
neither defines holiness nor separates it from other virtues. Indeed, on the basis of such "definition" holiness can no longer

even be called a virtue--since the gods are no longer restricted to loving only what is good for men--and men can have no rational motivation, other than fearing divine retribution, to do what is holy. And, of course, lacking any knowledge of what the gods might or might not love at any moment, men would have no way even to attempt conforming to the gods' unknown and unknowable will even if they should wish to do so. Moreover all such wish, and all fear of divine retribution, would be without any rational basis. For if we know nothing about divine loves and hates we do not even know whether the gods love or hate or in any way care about anything men do. To believe that they might would be as much a matter of ungrounded faith as it would be to deny it.

The conclusion of these arguments is therefore that the adoption of the alternative simply deprives the concept of all concrete, specifiable meaning and thus of all conceivable practical or theoretical significance.

Although these conclusions concerning the special domain of holiness or piety are already implicit in Euthyphro Part I, they are, as we shall see, further reinforced by the rest of the dialogue whose function is precisely this reinforcement which provides the connecting link between Euthyphro Part I and Part II.

Notes

1. No literal translation of to men...dia touto phileitai can convey Plato's point which is to distinguish between two kinds of things: a) the kind of things that are "loved"--belong in the class of beloved things--by virtue of the fact that someone happens to love them, for whatever reason, right or wrong, and b) the kind of things that are loved, when and if they happen to be loved, because and for the very reason that they are lovable, worthy of love, in themselves and on their own account, i.e. by virtue of possessing some characteristic that induces, attracts and commands the love of the wise lover, the lover who is astute enough to perceive this characteristic in the object.

2. As we shall see in Part II, even this is not likely to be conceded by Socrates although so far he has not argued against the stipulation but used it dialectically for the purpose of showing its uselessness for defining what is holy.

3. Even if in the stipulation that the gods love all that is fair and good and just we equate fair, good, just and holy, this does not mean that the gods do not love anything in addition to these things.

4. E.g. Cohen in Vlastos, The Philosophy of Socrates p. 175; Hoerber, "Plato's Euthyphro" pp. 104ff.; Th. Gomperz, Greek

Thinkers II p. 366; Allen, Plato's Euthyphro pp. 44-5.

5. In fact "resemblance" is, as we have seen, a most problematic term here. For not knowing what it was that the gods loved in the particular cases described, i.e. what aspect of the act or thing made it lovable to them, we could never know what resemblance might be relevant and therefore should be focussed upon in decisions based on the precedents they are supposed to "resemble".

6. In the section on Historical Background.

7. In that the ruler still wills and commands whatever he considers beneficial to himself and thus his will is still curtailed and the objects he is likely to will are still definable independently of his actual willing them and he still wills and commands them because he believes them to have a certain characteristic ("beneficial to him") rather than v. v.

8. And even the Republic's omission of piety from the list of cardinal virtues need not be interpreted as such indication, as we shall see (Postscript).

Aporetic Interlude (11B-E)

The first part of the dialogue ends aporetically, in a manner
all too familiar from other early Platonic dialogues: Socrates'
interlocutor admits his inability to define what is to be defined
and what he so confidently claimed to know. In this particular
case, as in the Meno, this admission is accompanied by a complaint about Socrates' method of questioning and its effect on
the person subjected to it.

Socrates: Now, if you please, do not keep me in the
dark but start all over again and tell me
what holiness really is, whether it is loved
by the gods or whatever else befalls it; we
will not quarrel about that. Just tell me
readily what is holiness and unholiness.

Euthyphro: But Socrates, I do not know how to say what
I mean. For somehow whatever we put forward
just keeps going around and does not want to
stay where we put it.

So: Your statements, Euthyphro, are like my an-
cestor's, Daedalus', creations. And had I
made them and laid them down you might blame
it on my relationship to him that my verbal
creations run away and do not want to stay
where they are put. But as it is the statements are yours and so some other jest is
needed, for as you yourself perceive they do
not want to stay still.

Eu: On the contrary, the jest seems quite appropriate to me, Socrates, for it is not I who
make these statements move about and not
stay put but you seem to be the Daedalus who
does that; were it for me they would have
stayed fixed.

So: Then I must be an even greater artist than he
was, for he could only make his own works
move about while I seem to do this to my own
as well as others'. And what is most ingen-
ious about my art is that I am skilled
against my will, for I would rather have my
words stay fixed and unmoving than possess
the art of Daedalus and Tantalus' wealth as
well.

Euthyphro's and Socrates' comments on the perplexity in which

89

Euthyphro finds himself tell us a great deal about the Socratic method itself as it is used in this and other early dialogues. For the reason that Euthyphro's proposed definitions do not stay still but run around is not just that they are wrong but that they are opinions uncritically accepted by Euthyphro on someone else's authority--in this case on that of popular traditional morality. Correct opinions accepted on the same basis could withstand the Socratic elenchus no better. For what alone would make them firm and immovable is the type of critical reflection that fastens one's beliefs by a chain of reasoning, and thus securely grounding them in indubitable first principles turns them into knowledge.[1] Though Socrates' claim that it is against his will that Euthyphro's opinions do not stay put is ironic--since the aim of the elenctic is precisely to set such beliefs in motion by shaking the believer's uncritical faith in them--his affirmation that what he most wants is definitions that stay firm and unswayable even under the most rigorous questioning is quite sincere. But such definitions being the result of critical reflection, the elenctic questioning that destroys the interlocutor's ungrounded faith and, it is hoped, starts him thinking for himself and on his own is the only aid the teacher can provide the student in his progress toward knowledge. It is precisely because Socrates wants to help his interlocutors acquire knowledge rather than merely another opinion accepted on someone else's, be it even Socrates' own, authority that in spite of his knowledge (of holiness) Socrates cannot engage in positive instruction but has to use the negative method he is using exclusively in this dialogue and its companion pieces.

What is most interesting in the juxtaposition of Euthyphro's and Socrates' methods of coming to conclusions is the coincidence of their form and content, i.e. of the form of the process of acquisition and the content actually acquired in each case. For Euthyphro, like Meletus and all orthodox Athenians, not only proceeds uncritically and accepts what he accepts--a definition of holiness--on someone else's authority rather than on that of his own critical thinking, but what he accepts--the definition--still leaves all concrete determination of the thing in question--what is and what is not holy in any particular case--to someone else's authority. Euthyphro's definition of holiness as what is god-loved remains, at least in its extreme form (what is holy is holy because it is god-loved), utterly authoritarian and heteronomous: it is still the gods' inscrutable love that alone determines what is and what is not holy, and Euthyphro on his own is as incapable of making independent decisions in matters of holiness after accepting the definition as he was apparently incapable of coming to a definition on his own in the first place.

The acceptance, on traditional authority, of the gods' sole authority for determining what is holy is in fact even more

circular than it already seems. For what the gods love and hate
is in the end determined for the orthodox believer not by any direct access to the gods themselves by way of a private epiphany—
Euthyphro's claims to be a seer and a prophet are greeted with
derision by the masses (3B-C) because they smack of unorthodoxy--
but simply by traditional popular belief. It is ultimately the
city's mythopoetic tradition, sanctioned by long-standing acceptance, that gives the concept of holiness whatever concrete
content it has. So all that Euthyphro has done was in effect to
move around in a circle. The definition he accepted from popular
religious tradition merely refers him back to popular religious
tradition for guidance and makes him utterly dependent (materially) on the uncritical acceptance of that tradition which he so
uncritically accepted (formally) in the first place. Proceeding
in the manner he does he not only cannot progress toward knowledge.
All his movement is in effect a sham; a movement that can never
take him beyond the point where he began.

And this is precisely Socrates' point in the Euthyphro and
the reason behind the Socratic method of instruction employed
here and the other early dialogues: that the traditional method
of instruction, and the uncritical reliance on authority it promotes, lead the individual nowhere as far as the acquisition of
knowledge is concerned. Instead of liberating him and making him
autonomous--and a knower--they merely entangle him further and
further in their own unbreakable web. The orthodox believer, dis-
couraged from critical reflection by the authority of tradition,
remains a captive of tradition's self-reinforcing authority.

In contrast to this lack of movement out of and away from
utter heteronomy, the Socratic method really sets things in motion
simply because it sets autonomous thought in motion. In spite of
the fact that its form and content coincide just as much as those
of Euthyphro's method, and that in some ways this method is just
as circular as that of Euthyphro, the Socratic method, albeit no
less self-reinforcing than the traditional one, is anything but a
vicious circle.

What Socrates claims to want from, but in effect wants to
impart to, Euthyphro is knowledge. Since knowledge, unlike opinion, cannot be imparted heteronomously--by direct positive instruction the receiver is required to accept passively, relying
on the teacher's authority--but must be acquired by the learner
himself, the Socratic elenctic can start the student on the way to
knowledge only by weakening, if possible destroying, the hold of
tradition on him and thus making him free for, and hopefully inducing him to engage in, critical reflection.

And not only is knowledge the goal and critical reflection
the way to the goal of the Socratic method, but what is ultimately

91

known—or would be known by Euthyphro if he were capable of the critical reflection demanded of him—here, i.e. the concept of holiness, is itself properly defined as nothing but a type of knowledge. Nevertheless the knowledge that holiness is but a type of knowledge (of what is most wholesome or good) does not yet end the search for knowledge because it does not as yet give the student any concrete insight. On the contrary, it merely starts him on the search for concrete knowledge—of whatever is holy in the particular context in which he has to make a decision about holiness. Thus the Socratic method is as self-reinforcing as the traditional one. The critical reflection it induces in the learner leads to a result—a knowledge of what is holy as such—which induces further critical reflection—on what is holy in the given concrete situation. And this knowledge too can be acquired only by the knower's own effort, the same as the knowledge—of the form of holiness—that he already acquired in this manner.

So, in a way, the Socratic method is, where it works, as circular and self-reinforcing as the method it combats. It requires autonomy of thought as the only way to acquire the knowledge (of the concept of holiness) sought for, and it shows that this knowledge requires further autonomous thought for the actual possession of the virtue now known. Whoever is started on this road is just as inevitably caught in its web as those who cannot break the hold of tradition are held fast by it.

Nevertheless there is a world of difference between these two methods as far as their particular results are concerned. For the Socratic method makes the individual a captive of his own critical thought and this 'captivity' is tantamount to freedom, the freedom of thought that autonomous reflection provides and guarantees. Thus the Socratic elenchus, by forcing the individual to think for himself, in effect liberates the individual as thinker. The circle he is caught in is the circle of his own autonomous thought. For a man of intelligence this is surely the healthiest of circles.

Furthermore, the circularity of thought we have so far observed is merely a formal aspect of the aim and method of Socratic education. There is another way in which the Socratic method involves the learner in a circular inquiry: the knowledge he acquires by his own search not only induces him to search for further knowledge, but all the knowledge he acquires and searches for here is ultimately nothing but knowledge of himself: a knowledge of his own nature, function and good, a knowledge of what is truly wholesome and good for himself by nature. Thus the knowledge acquired or to be acquired here is not only self-acquired, it is also self-knowledge. The knower and the known, subject and object of the inquiry, are one and the same when it comes to the only type of knowledge Socrates is concerned with in the Euthyphro and its companion dialogues: the knowledge of, the knowledge that is,

92

human excellence.

And this is what must be emphasized here lest it appear that because of its formal circularity the Socratic method is indeed as empty, lacking in all substantial content, and neither promising nor capable of delivering any actual product, as some interpreters seem to think. For what we must not forget in dealing with the Euthyphro and kindred dialogues is that its, and their, subject is virtue. And this is neither an indifferent type of knowledge nor a knowledge men are incapable of acquiring.

It is not indifferent knowledge, as we have seen, for virtue being that by virtue of which eudaimonia, self-fulfillment, human happiness is attained, no man can be indifferent to its possession. Knowing what it is, formally, and knowing that he does not yet have it in fact, each individual will necessarily strive for its concrete possession.

But knowing what virtue is—knowledge of good and evil, self-knowledge—he also knows how to go about acquiring it—by his own reflection on his own nature and of the world in which he lives. Thus a (formal) knowledge of virtue necessarily leads to the (actual, material) acquisition of virtue; a knowledge of what human excellence is makes a man excellent in the end. This knowledge is far from "unproductive"; its product is the only product every man by nature necessarily desires to possess: human excellence in the sense of doing and faring well. Whoever comes to know what is truly virtuous—holy and good—grows not only in knowledge but in being, i.e. in being what he by nature is. He improves not just his intellect but his life. He moves not merely toward insight but, by virtue of this insight into himself, toward self-fulfillment. As a self-moved mover (moved by his autonomous thought revealing to him the necessity for autonomous thought) he moves toward himself in two ways at once: toward himself as the object of the inquiry (what am I, what is truly holy and unholy, wholesome and destructive, for me?) and toward himself (the full self, the well-functioning self, the self as it truly ought to be) as the ultimate object of the movement.

Circular this movement may be in that its subject, object and method coincide, but unlike Euthyphro's entanglement in tradition the circle here is the opposite of being vicious. Autonomous thought is the only thing that cures the soul both of ignorance and of unessential, inauthentic existence. This is precisely what makes it itself "holy", i.e. truly wholesome: a purification of, indeed the sole safe and sound means of purifying, human life. And this is what makes the heteronomy Socrates combats so unholy and unwholesome: discouraging autonomous thought the rule of tradition tends to prevent rather than promote the purity, health and well-functioning of the orthodox individual and his society. In the manner of an Aeschylean hero's attempt at purifying of blood-pollution by the further shedding of blood, orthodox "thinking" merely pollutes what it seeks to purify.

Of course Euthyphro is, as his complaint indicates and as Socrates repeatedly points out in the following sections (11E, 12E), as indolent a thinker, and therefore as inept a subject for Socratic instruction as were the Athenians themselves in real life. Lacking the ability to engage in the critical thinking that alone could make any of them autonomous as well as truly virtuous, he and they merely blamed Socrates for trying to subvert their heteronomy by uprooting and setting into motion what tradition established on seemingly firm ground and wanted to preserve unshaken.

But at this point, and indeed all along in the Euthyphro, it is not a matter of Euthyphro's or the Athenian public's instruction. Plato did not present Euthyphro, and Socrates did not consider the Athenian public at large, endowed with enough intelligence to be corrigible. It is to the philosophically minded, or at least potentially philosophical, audience that Socrates is speaking in the dialogue. And so, since Euthyphro is unable to really free himself from the opinions he is clearly incapable of defending, and having been forcibly deprived of them has no idea of how to continue the inquiry, Socrates proceeds to take over the immediate direction of the discussion and himself suggests a new way of departure.[2]

Notes

1. See Meno 97D-98A.

2. The structure of the dialogue is analogous here to that of the Meno where Meno's Euthyphro-like complaints are followed by Socrates proposing a hypothesis as an aid for carrying on the inquiry.

11E-13A Socrates: Enough of this. Since you seem to be so lazy I will come to your aid so you may teach me about what is holy. Just do not give up before we are finished. Rather consider whether you believe that whatever is holy is also necessarily just.

Euthyphro: I do.

So: And is whatever just also holy? Or is whatever is holy just but all that is just not necessarily holy, only part of it holy and part something else?

Eu: I do not follow what you say, Socrates.

So: And yet you are no less younger than you are wiser than I; only, as I said, your wealth of wisdom has made you indolent. Now exert yourself my friend, for it is not hard to understand what I mean. What I am saying is the opposite of what the poet uttered:

> Do not name Zeus, the creator and sustainer of all;
> For where there is fear there is also reverence.

I disagree with the poet on this. Shall I tell you why?

Eu: Please do.

So: It does not seem to me that wherever there is fear there is also reverence, for I think many people who are afraid of sickness and poverty and the like do indeed fear them but in no way revere what they fear. Do you not think so?

Eu: I do.

So: But where there is reverence there is also fear; for does not anyone who feels reverence and shame about an act also fear and dread an evil reputation?

Eu: He does.

95

So: Then it is not right to say that where there
       is fear there is also reverence; rather,
       where there is reverence there is also fear
       but where there is fear there is not always
       reverence. Fear is a more inclusive term
       than reverence; reverence is, as it were, a
       part of fear, just as odd numbers are a
       part of all numbers and therefore where there
       are numbers there is not necessarily an odd
       number but where there is an odd number there
       is also number as such. Do you follow me
       now?

Eu: Yes.

So: Well it was this sort of thing I meant when
       I asked whether it is the case that whatever
       is just is also necessarily holy, or is it
       rather that whatever is holy is also just
       but what is just is not always holy because
       what is holy is merely a part of what is
       just. Shall we assert the latter or do you
       disagree?

Eu: No, I agree; I think the latter statement is
       correct.

So: Well then consider this. If what is holy is
       only a part of what is just, we ought, it
       seems, to find out what part. As in the pre-
       vious case, for example, if you had asked me
       what part of all numbers even numbers were
       and what is an even number like I would have
       answered that even numbers are divisible by
       two rather than being indivisible in this
       manner; or do you not agree?

Eu: I do.

So: Well then do try to show me in this way what
       part of justice holiness is, so I can tell
       Meletus not to do me an injustice nor indict
       me for impiety, for I have been adequately
       instructed by you about what is pious and
       holy and what is not.

Eu: This is what I think, then, Socrates: that
       piety and holiness are the part of justice
       which has to do with our attending to the
       gods (therapeia theōn), and the remaining

96

part has to do with our attending to men.

So: Now that seems an excellent answer,
                Euthyphro.

The problem to which Socrates turns here is the one we
touched upon in discussing the conclusions implicit in Part I:
What if anything distinguishes holiness from the rest of virtue?
What is the special domain of holiness, if indeed there is such a
domain? This problem arises quite naturally in the context of the
dialogue. Since the implicit conclusion of Part I seemed to be that
what is holy is just about synonymous with what is good, and
therefore holiness is just about equivalent with virtue as such,
the question Socrates raises here is a way of testing the truth
of that conclusion.

Why Socrates picks justice as the particular virtue whose
relation to piety is to be used as a test case is not too important for us. One reason might be that justice and piety are the
virtues that have been most frequently and most closely associated
with each other by tradition—as they were also in Euthyphro's
own tradition-based arguments (e.g. 4B, 6A, 8Bff.). Another
might be that while eusebeia as a kind of fear or reverence strongly resembles courage (itself defined as a kind of fear in the
Laches and the Republic) and temperance (as aidos, a kind of fear
and reverence), the term justice does not create such literal
resonances and therefore its identity with piety might seem the
easiest to contest. Be this as it may, the choice of justice in
particular is immaterial if the arguments that follow turn out to
be equally relevant to the problem of the relationship between
piety and any other virtue, indeed virtue as such.

The question Socrates raises is whether holiness and justice
are coextensive terms so that all things holy are at the same time
also just and v. v., as e.g. things evil and things to be feared
are one and the same (Laches 198B); or is it rather the case that
justice is a wider, more inclusive term containing holiness as
one of its parts, as e.g. the term "number" is wider than the
term "odd number" and includes the latter as a subset.

Euthyphro opts for the second alternative—that piety is a
narrower term than justice and the class of all just acts includes
the class of all holy ones as a subset—and Socrates readily
agrees. This agreement is, as we shall see, purely dialectical
at this point; Euthyphro's proposal is accepted by Socrates merely as a hypothesis to be tested. The ensuing discussion alone
will reveal whether the hypothesis happens to be tenable or not.[1]

With the agreement made the elenchus can now begin. Accepting the hypothesis that holiness is but a part of justice, i.e.

that justice has a wider domain of application than holiness and includes the latter's domain as a part of its more extensive one, Socrates can now ask Euthyphro to specify what exactly the domain of holiness is as a part of that of justice. What follows is a series of closely connected arguments which prove each of Euthyphro's successive attempts to specify the proper, restricted domain of holiness to be untenable.

Note

1. Such dialectical assents—Socrates provisorically agreeing to some statement regardless of whether he holds it to be true—are a commonplace in the early dialogues. In the Laches e.g. Socrates himself suggests that courage is a part rather than the whole of virtue, yet upon investigation this suggestion turns out to be irreconcilable with the definition of courage which we know Socrates himself held to be true (and which is ironically rejected at the end of the Laches in order that the dialogue end in aporia). That Socrates' acceptance of the hypothesis here in the Euthyphro may be merely dialectical is also suggested by the fact that in other dialogues he is quite willing to argue the opposite of what he agrees to here. In the Protagoras e.g. where the relationship of the various virtues to each other is discussed Socrates maintains that justice and holiness are much the same thing (dikaiosune hoion hosiotes kai he hosiotes hoion dikaiosune 331B), and all that is holy is at the same time just while all that is just is at the same time holy. Clearly both statements, Euthyphro's here and Socrates' in the Protagoras, cannot be right, and so we must at least leave the possibility open that Socrates' agreement with Euthyphro here is somewhat less than heartfelt.

13A-B	Socrates:	There is, however, one little point on which I need more information, for I do not quite understand what you mean by "attending". For you are not saying, I suppose, that attending to the gods is just like attending to anything else. We say for instance that not everyone knows how to attend to horses but only the skilled horseman, is that not right?
	Euthyphro:	It is.
	So:	And so horsemanship is the art of attending to horses?
	Eu:	Yes.
	So:	Nor does everyone know how to attend to dogs, but only the huntsman.
	Eu:	Right.
	So:	And huntsmanship is the art of attending to dogs?
	Eu:	Yes.
	So:	And the oxherd's art is that of attending to oxen?
	Eu:	Of course.
	So:	Holiness and piety are then the art of attending to the gods, Euthyphro; is that what you are saying?
	Eu:	Yes.
	So:	And does not all attending accomplish the same thing, such as bringing about some good or benefit for whatever is attended to, the way you see that horses are benefited and improved when attended to by horsemen; or do you not think so?
	Eu:	I do.
	So:	And dogs by huntsmen and oxen by oxherds, and everything else likewise? Or do you think that attending ever aims at injuring

99

75004

	what is attended to?
Eu:	No, by god, I do not.
So:	At benefiting then?
Eu:	Of course.
So:	Then holiness, being the art of attending to the gods, benefits and improves the gods; and you would agree that whenever you do something holy you improve some of the gods?
Eu:	No, by god, I would not.
So:	Nor do I think that is what you mean Euthyphro; far from it. That is exactly why I asked what you meant by attending to the gods, because I did not think that was what you were saying.
Eu:	And you were right, Socrates; I do not mean anything like that.

Euthyphro's first attempt to define the special domain of holiness is as traditional and orthodox as is just about everything he says in the dialogue. And the attempt fails because its definition (literally de-limiting, drawing boundaries around what is to be defined) is incoherent with at least one other traditional belief that Euthyphro seems to be unwilling to relinquish. So once again Euthyphro's failure is not altogether his own; it is the result of the inconsistency of traditional religious beliefs which the Socratic questioning helps to reveal.

In Euthyphro's opinion the part of justice which as holiness is distinguishable from the rest is the part concerned with our therapeia of the gods. Whatever involves such therapy is both just and pious, while all other acts lie outside the domain of piety, however just they may be otherwise.

Although therapeia in Greek may mean "service", this connotation of the word will receive special attention in the section immediately following. To begin with Socrates focusses on therapeia only in the sense of tending to, taking care of, fostering, cultivating, healing, curing, restoring to its best state that which is the subject of therapeia.

Such therapy, as he immediately points out, is a matter of knowledge. As in the kindred arts of tending to horses, dogs or cattle not everyone but only the skilled craftsman knows what is

100

proper therapy (of horses, dogs, etc.) so the therapy of the gods too would have to depend on the (pious man's) knowledge of the proper ways of practicing this therapeutic activity. Should piety be any kind of therapy, a knowledge of some kind would be a necessary precondition of the possession of this virtue.

Therapy in the above sense is, furthermore, always directed at the improvement of whatever object it is practiced on. What the skilled therapist must know is simply how to foster, cultivate, cure, implement in or restore to its best possible state, what he treats. Thus all therapy presupposes that the thing or organism it is practiced on is not as it by nature ought to be—either it has not yet attained to its ideal state or it has declined from it; in any case it is in some way deficient in its functioning and falls short of fulfilling its function in the best possible way. This is, after all, why any type of therapy is invented, that the thing it is supposed to care for is not already, and is not likely to become if left to itself, as it ought to be; and the sole goal of the art is to improve it, provide for its needs and make it more excellent in the aspect of its being that the art is concerned with.

In view of this, therapy not only requires knowledge, but the type of knowledge it requires is always a knowledge of what is good: i.e. what is the natural aim, function, good of the thing or organism in question; what is good for, i.e. will promote, the attainment of this end; and how to go about arranging things in such a way that this goal is realized as well as it can possibly be. In speaking of therapy we are therefore merely talking about virtue in the widest sense; not just human virtue but virtue as such: that by virtue of which anything attains to its highest possible excellence.

This interpretation of the therapeutic arts, indeed of practical arts in general, is commonplace in Plato,[1] and since Socrates merely articulates the full implications of what therapy in one of its traditional senses means Euthyphro can hardly object to his interpretation. And this is what puts him on the horns of a dilemma.

Therapy in the above sense implies a lack of excellence, a deficient state of being and functioning, in whatever the therapy is practiced on; it is this lack of excellence that makes the thing needy of therapy, and it is this deficiency that the therapy is designed to alleviate. The practice of therapy implies furthermore that the therapist is in some sense superior to or more knowledgeable than its subject or patient,[2] in that he can do for the latter what it could not do for and by himself or itself. And these are the implications Euthyphro finds himself unable or unwilling to accept once Socrates points them out.

101

Although the traditional gods of Greek mythology were not conspicuously perfect and therefore incapable of improvement, they were nevertheless popularly regarded to be infinitely superior to, more powerful and wiser than men. Unlike human existence their life was thought to be excellent, blessed, and altogether happy; the quintessence of all men could aspire to and conceive of in their wildest dreams—hardly a state in need of or capable of great improvement, and least of all of improvement brought about by men coming to the aid of gods as practitioners of a kind of "divine therapy". Whether or not the Platonic Socrates shares this popular belief,3 he brings it into play dialectically to show its incompatibility with defining piety as a therapy of the gods in the sense so far discussed.

Faced with this incoherence, and unwilling to relinquish the traditional belief in the overall superiority, excellence, and altogether self-sufficient, happy existence of the gods, Euthyphro chooses to give up the attempt to delineate the domain of piety by means of the notion of a therapy of the gods in the sense specified and takes recourse to a sense of therapeia so far left out of account. This new connotation of therapeia is in fact much more in line with what the Greeks have always meant when they talked about a therapeia theōn (e.g. Od. 11,255; Erga 136). Nevertheless it proves to be as untenable, and for the same reasons, as did the previous one.

Notes

1. See e.g. Rep. I 341E-342E, 345D-347A; Apol. 24C-25C; Lysis 317A-B.

2. See the doctor/ruler analogy in Republic I (342C).

3. Statements such as Rep. 381B "God and everything that belongs to him is in its best possible state" and Symp. 202C-D to the effect that the gods are and possess all and lack nothing that is fair and good in no way imply that Socrates or Plato actually believed in the existence of such gods. In the Republic the above statement is made in the context of giving guidelines for the poetic education of the young and ignorant who could not be philosophically instructed and must therefore be guided by myths. And in the Symposium the point of emphasizing the gods' perfection is to prove that the gods are incapablé of love—an ironic commentary on Euthyphro's attempts at defining holiness in terms of what the gods love. We shall return to this later (pp. 120ff).

13D-14B	Socrates:	Fine. But then, what kind of attention to the gods is holiness?
	Euthyphro:	The kind, Socrates, that slaves pay in attending to their masters.
	So:	I see. It is a kind of servile attention to the gods, it seems.
	Eu:	Yes.
	So:	Now can you tell me what this kind of service serves to bring about when it is rendered to physicians? Is it not health?
	Eu:	It is.
	So:	And a service to shipbuilders, what does it serve to produce?
	Eu:	Obviously ships, Socrates.
	So:	And service to house-builders, houses?
	Eu:	Yes.
	So:	Well then, what does a service to the gods serve to bring about? You must know that, since you say you know more about matters of divinity than any other man.
	Eu:	And what I say is true, Socrates.
	So:	Then, by god, tell me what sublime work do the gods accomplish by using our services?
	Eu:	Many are the works, and fair too, Socrates.
	So:	Yes, and so are those of generals, too, my friend; yet you have no trouble asserting that their main work is to bring about victory in war. Right?
	Eu:	Right.
	So:	And farmers, too, accomplish many things and fair; just the same their main work is to produce food from the earth?
	Eu:	Quite.

103

So: Well then, of the many and fair works the
          gods accomplish, what is the main product of
          their activity?

Eu: I told you a little while ago, Socrates, that
          it would take a lot of work to learn about
          all these things.

Euthyphro has focussed on a sense of therapeia so far neglected: submissively attending, waiting on, serving in a subordinate position whoever is being attended to in this kind of therapy. Piety, he now says, is hyperetike: the kind of service
slaves and menial servants perform for their masters. Unlike the
previous sense of therapeia, hyperetike no longer implies any superiority on the part of the person rendering it. On the contrary
it suggests a decidedly inferior status; it is hard labor engaged
in by an inferior being who performs in almost unquestioning obe-
dience what his master bids him to do. As such hyperetike no
longer seems to require any type of higher skill or special knowledge on the part of the person performing it; the most it presupposes, in the strict sense of the word, is some kind of menial
strength and ability to carry out the master's commands.

Although this definition of piety as a kind of slavish, ignorant, and utterly submissive hyperetike theon would, if taken seriously, fatally undercut Euthyphro's and the city's claim to know
and thus to be able to prescribe whatever is holy in each case,
and thus leave the pious man in the same position as the definition previously rejected (what is holy is holy because it is god-
loved), instead of merely repeating the previous arguments Socrates attacks the definition by questioning the very concept of hyperetike as applied to our direct relationship to the gods themselves. His attack follows a line closely related to that of the
previous argument against the notion of divine therapy.

Hyperetike as the kind of service specified may not imply as
a precondition of its performance a great deal of knowledge on the
part of the servant who merely follows the directions of his superior without questioning or understanding their whys and wherefores.
But it does imply that these superiors themselves have a kind of
work or activity, a work in which the servant assists them through
his inferior, menial type of labor.

A doctor's work, e.g. serves to bring about the health of the
patient (and is, therefore, the kind of therapy previously discussed), and whoever assists the doctor in this work helps him accomplish precisely this end, i.e. the improvement of the patient's
health. Likewise, a ship-builder's servant becomes a however inferior co-worker of the ship-builder and helps him do his work better and with greater ease than he could do it without such assistance.

On this analogy already the master--in this case the god served--is less than altogether self-sufficient, i.e. sufficient to performing his essential task, since he needs and can profit from the servant's help; at least he is less efficient at doing the work entirely by himself than with the assistance of his co-worker. And so the master is, in fact, to some extent, benefited by his servant's activity, which is precisely what Euthyphro was unwilling to grant in the previous argument.

But the chief shortcoming of Euthyphro's conception of hyper-etike is that he is unable to specify what exactly the special ac-tivity or work of the gods is whose performance constitutes their essential nature in the way a doctor, shipbuilder or any kind of craftsman is defined in the strict sense--i.e. qua doctor, etc.-- by the special work he alone performs or performs better than any-one else. Faced with this question concerning the essential work or function of the gods qua gods, the special function whose ful-fillment constitutes their very being, Euthyphro is at a loss as to what to say.

But lacking any insight into the gods' special nature and function, how could he, or anyone, claim to know what is and what is not holy, i.e. what does and what does not serve the gods in the fulfillment of their function? How could one therefore know what hyperetike might consist in, and being ignorant of this how could anyone intelligently engage in hyperetike?

Even when the later Plato admits[1] the possibility of some kind of divine inspiration revealing to men what they on their own could not know, he is careful enough to point out the dangers in-herent in blindly relying on this type of rare and privileged com-munication. For in the absence of any insight into the nature, essential function or work of the gods, how could anyone ever tell what particular commands do in fact come from a god and which others have their source in a merely human aberration, an unhealth-y, unwholesome and unholy fit of madness possessing the individual and driving him out of his mind? Whether or not Plato is serious in what he says about divine madness in the Phaedrus, he does not negelct to emphasize that there are types of madness that are mere-ly human or subhuman rather than divine, and so madness as such is not by itself a sign of holiness and a more than human wisdom for him. And which it is in each case, obviously no ignorant tool of a possibly more, possibly less than human inspiration is ever in a position to know. (This is what Kierkegaard so conveniently ig-nores in extolling Abraham's divine madness).

At any rate, such are the consequences of Euthyphro's defini-tion of piety as hyperetike as long as Euthyphro remains incapable of specifying the very criteria of divinity by articulating what he considers to be the gods' essential nature and function. Since

whatever may or may not be man's proper service to the gods is
left undefined here, the 'definition' is useless for distinguishing piety from justice, a supposedly more inclusive term. Indeed,
since by itself it does not even help us distinguish pious, i.e.
god-serving, acts from any other type of action no matter how unjust and vicious such behavior may be in human eyes, the 'definition' does not even insure piety's being a virtue. Euthyphro's
'knowledge' of piety is once again revealed to be a sham. Hyperetike of some kind Euthyphro may or may not be engaged in. But
that his slavish and ignorant service to something he fails to
comprehend is virtuous he can no longer claim.

Though Euthyphro is clearly ignorant of whatever the gods'
proper work or function may be, and therefore, quite rightly,
abandons the notion of hyperetike and goes on to define piety as a
kind of prayer and sacrifice, it is worth considering at this
point what if anything the Platonic Socrates may have regarded to
be the essential work and function of the gods. For a number of
interpreters consider the section we are dealing with to be central to the interpretation of the whole dialogue. Noting that the
definition of piety as hyperetike is the only one proposed that is
not actually refuted in the Euthyphro, and taking at face value
Socrates' comment on Euthyphro's failure to continue the discussion of hyperetike--"It is plain that you are not willing to instruct me. For just now, when you were so close to it, you turned
away. Had you but answered, I would have forthwith learned from
you all there is to learn about holiness" (14B-C)--they use the
preceding section as a clue for finding the positive, substantive
message of the Euthyphro.

Although I would regard Socrates' comment as ironical--for
reasons to be elaborated below--and consider the principle of interpretation that the positions taken and left finally unrefuted
represent, or must be used to infer, Socrates' positive doctrines[2]
altogether bizarre when applied to a Socratic dialogue,[3] it is instructive to take a brief look at these interpretations and see
what evidence there is in the early dialogues to support them.

Following Bonitz, who identifies the essential nature of the
gods with the Republic's Idea of the Good, Heidel, Krueger, Arnim,
Raeder and Gauss[4] come to rather similar conclusions. Since, according to them, the work of the gods consists in the realization
of the Good in the world, true piety as men's service to the gods
is nothing other than men's cooperation with the gods in realizing
the Good in whatever way this can be accomplished by men. Chief
among these ways would be the improvement of the human soul, on
which improvement all other goods for men depend. Since this improvement is precisely the acquisition of human excellence, piety,
as men's service to and cooperation with the gods, is in fact
nothing but virtue as such.

Even Rabinowitz, who in my view rightly objects to importing the Idea of the Good from the Republic into the Euthyphro, and insists that "no evidence exists within the entire Platonic corpus to suggest that theos ever denoted the idea of the good or the causal agent thereof",[5] ends up with a not altogether different conclusion. Basing his interpretation on the Timaeus, Laws, Philebus and the Republic, he identifies divine essence with Reason, declares the work or function of the gods to be noesis as "the apprehension of the Platonic ideas" (fn. p.117), and concludes by equating piety with philosophy as such. "...the only art capable of aiding them (the gods) to perform this function must be (the) Platonic art of philosophical dialectic". "God is nous and genuine piety (is) philosophy".[6]

My main methodological objection to all these interpretations, including Rabinowitz', is that they rely just about exclusively on dialogues much later than the Euthyphro and the other early Platonic writings, and import into the Euthyphro ideas which Socrates, on the basis of the evidence of the Socratic dialogues, cannot be shown to have held.[7]

As for substantive objections, they can be best elaborated by considering what would follow from these interpreations if one entertained them seriously in the context of the Euthyphro. Do they in fact succeed in turning Euthyphro's definition of piety as hyperetike theōn into something useful and viable?

What is evident right away is that none of these attempts contribute anything to solving Euthyphro's immediate problem which is to delineate the domain of piety within the larger domain of justice. For if the essential function and chief work of the gods is the realization of the Good, the rational end of all (divine and human) activity, then piety as hyperetike theōn is in fact the whole of virtue and not just a part (or a part of a part, i.e. justice). And while this objection would not necessarily invalidate Euthyphro's definition itself—which would now be a definition of virtue as such—the next one is more serious: All the suggested interpretations result in making the definition of piety as hyperetike theōn at best redundant, at worst paradoxical if not self-contradictory.

If divine nature is identified with the Good, or with teleological Reason aiming at the realization of the Good in the world, and therefore the chief work and essential function of the gods, the work in which men can assist them through their service, is the fostering of goodness through philosophical activity aimed at human improvement, then any reference to the gods in the definition of piety becomes entirely gratuitous. For what is good—contributory to human excellence, the rational end of men as teleological beings—we either know by the exercise of our own reason—and not by reference to and through dependence on divine

Reason--and in that case we know it independently of any knowledge of divine nature and function. Or else we do not know and are on our own incapable of knowing it, and in that case no reference to the gods--whose nature and function is now defined precisely by what we do not and cannot know--is of any help whatever. Since the gods have become here a mere surrogate for rationality, human reason either suffices for doing the job--knowing and doing what is holy, supremely rational or good--by itself and entirely on its own, or else it does not suffice even for identifying what is divine--rational, good--and what therefore might constitute hyperetike theōn, the type of cooperation with the gods that would promote the realization of divine purpose in the world.

Thus the kind of quasi-Kantian restoration of the autonomy of human reason that this interpretation brings with it--that it is our knowledge of what is moral, rational, or good that enables us to identify what is divine in the first place--simply eliminates all vestiges of and need for the kind of heteronomy that Euthyphro's theological definition of piety as hyperetike theōn implies. And not only is a reference to the gods on this interpretation superfluous for finding out what men ought to do to be pious, but it is also totally unnecessary for the purpose of providing motivation for men performing this type of "service". For the work specified--the realization of what is good, through the proper exercise of human reason--is quite apart from its allegedly being the essence of divinity, by definition also the essence of human rationality. Thus by itself, i.e. by its own teleological nature, human reason has already the strongest possible motivation to perform it; in doing so, it is, after all, merely fulfilling its own function and accomplishing its own natural good. According to the Socratic arguments we already rehearsed, no man can rationally wish to do anything other or less than precisely this.

So far I have argued merely that the interpretations discussed make all reference to the gods in the definition of piety redundant. If this is so, however, then the notion of hyperetike itself becomes paradoxical if not self-contradictory. For hyperetike in the sense discussed in this section of the dialogue means a kind of almost slavish service performed at the behest of and under the exclusive direction of a superior being whose reasons for commanding such acts the servant does not and need not comprehend. But here, i.e. if we follow the line of argument suggested, such assymetrical relation of superiority/inferiority no longer obtains. It is now man's autonomous reason rather than a god's superior insight that reveals what the work to be performed is, and in performing it men serve first and foremost themselves and accomplish their ends, rather than submit to someone else and subordinate their ends to his. While serving oneself is not necessarily incompatible with serving, at the same time, others whose ends happen to coincide with one's own, this type of relationship is very far from being hyperetike in the strict sense. It is, at the very least, more a relationship between equals than one of subordinates to superiors.

In fact, the relationship of subordination Euthyphro meant to talk about is just about reversed on this interpretation. For if the gods' essential function and chief work is the cultivation of human excellence, then are not the gods in effect our servants, subservient to our purposes? In pretending to serve them do we not in fact merely use them as tools and instruments of our own self-fulfillment, so that the very notion of divine service turns into a sham here, and becomes the kind of hypocritical, self-serving, though no less useful lie that Critias so ably satirized? (On the other hand, should the gods' chief work and function be something other than the accomplishing of what is good for men, then helping them to accomplish their essential work we would fail to accomplish ours, and such hyperetike theōn could not then be any part of virtue, i.e. that by virtue of which the human agent improves and fulfills his own life).

Quite apart from this subversion and inversion of Euthyphro's notion of hyperetike, there is a further problem with defining piety as any kind of assistance to or cooperation with the essential activity or work of the gods themselves. Euthyphro's previous definition of piety as therapeia theōn had to be abandoned because Euthyphro was not willing to concede that the gods could be improved or benefited in any way by our activity. But this reluctance of Euthyphro's is equally fatal to the notion of hyperetike. For our helpfully assisting the gods in the performance of their own essential and chief work would inevitably improve their functioning and thus their very being which consists in the performance of their essential function. Therefore the notion of hyperetike is fully as incompatible with the belief in the perfection of the gods, or, at least, in their non-perfectibility by men, as was the notion of therapeia in the preceding section.

And this is not just a matter of Euthyphro's and the orthodox Athenians' possibly incoherent beliefs. To the extent that Socrates or Plato can be said to have had any opinion on the subject[8] it is unlikely that they regarded divine nature in its truest sense to be any more improvable than did Euthyphro. E.g. if one decided to take seriously passages like Republic 381B-C and Symposium 202C-D which declare the gods to be always already in their best possible state, in possession of all that is good and fair, and being neither capable of nor in need of improvement to abide in the state forever, one would have to conclude that Plato himself regarded the gods incapable of improvement.

On this view, however, all interpretations of hyperetike

109

theōn become untenable. Rabinowitz' interpretation, according to which it is philosophical activity that we can share with the gods, is incoherent with Symp. 203E-204A where it is argued that the gods being perfectly wise neither desire nor seek wisdom and thus cannot conceivably engage in philosophical activity. And so is every suggestion, as to what the gods' chief work in which we could assist them might be, incompatible with the gods' presumed perfection. For if the gods are indeed incapable of improvement in any way, then it is strictly speaking impossible that they could rationally engage in any kind of activity either by themselves or in collaboration with us. Rational activity in Plato is necessarily teleological: directed at the accomplishment of one's own end and good. But if the gods are always already as good as possible and possessed of all that is good for them, then their rational end, the greatest possible fulfillment of their own nature and function, is always already fully accomplished. They can have no ends still outstanding, no good yet to be attained, and thus no rational motivation for action. They simply cannot conceivably have any erga to perform, and thus there can be no divine activity in whose performance we could assist the gods. The idea of the gods' perfection is in every way incompatible with the possibility of a human hyperetike theōn.[9]

The overall result of the preceding considerations is that Euthyphro's definition of piety as hyperetike breaks down and proves to be untenable no matter how we choose to interpret this section of the dialogue. Whether Euthyphro is unable to specify what exactly the gods' essential function and chief work is merely because of his own ignorance of divine nature, or because the gods, being unimprovable, cannot have any essential activity at all, lacking such specification he can have no idea of what hyperetike theōn might consist in and thus his 'definition' fails to provide a paradigm--something he can actually use for the determination of what is and what is not holy. And even if we ignore the difficulties with assigning any essential activity to presumably perfect gods and try to specify divine activity along the line of Bonitz' and others' well meant attempts, hyperetike theōn still remains an extremely dubious notion. It inverts into its opposite the very relation (hyperetike) it asserts to be piety, it makes all reference to the gods superfluous and uninformative, and it fails to show piety to be a part rather than the whole of human excellence. Thus in the end it does not matter at all whether we regard--or the Platonic Socrates ever regarded--the essence of divinity to be knowable by men; the concept of hyperetike theōn in both its parts--qua hyperetike as well as in its reference to the gods--turns out to be thoroughly unilluminating; it is at best useless at worst contradictory.

That Euthyphro is aware of all these considerations is doubtful. At any rate, and for whatever reason--the one he pleads is shortness of time--he abandons the notion of hyperetike and tries to provide another definition.

Notes

1. In the Phaedrus. That the Meno's conclusions about virtue being a divine gift, the result of divinely inspired right opinion, are obviously ironical I argued before (Philosophical Presuppositions) and will return to later (n. 3).

2. Heidel, Plato's Euthyphro p. 20: "In recent years a principle governing the interpretation of the dialogues of Plato has obtained among scholars almost universal recognition. It may be thus stated: In determining the positive doctrine which Plato desired the reader to infer from the argument of any dialogue, we must take for our point of departure the position taken and finally left unrefuted".

3. Instead of rehearsing all the arguments against using this principle for ascertaining what Socrates really means in a dialogue where the Socratic method--negative, ironic, elenctic, maieutic, aporetic--is conspicuously employed, I will merely point to the paradoxical consequences of using the principle for interpreting one such dialogue. In the Meno (99B-100A) the only position "taken and finally left unrefuted" is that virtue is a kind of divinely inspired right opinion accepted without comprehension by those who happen to be thus divinely inspired and possessed. That this position is totally irreconcilable with Socrates' actual teaching--that virtue is knowledge--in the early and middle dialogues is hardly worth mentioning. One might note, however, that it is also a position diametrically opposed to the one that Heidel, following this principle, attributes to Socrates as his "real message" in the Euthyphro. See e.g. Heidel's comment on Euth. 10A: "the argument virtually means that the essence of holiness is independent of the will of the deity, that is to say, that the human spirit is as truly autonomous in the field of religion as in the field of philosophical truth generally, where it has always asserted its independence" (Plato's Euthyphro p. 68).

4. Bonitz, Platonische Studien pp. 233-34; G. Krueger, Werke des Aufstiegs p. 272; Heidel, TAPA 31/1900 pp. 173ff., Plato's Euthyphro p. 84; Arnim, Platons Jugenddialoge pp. 199ff.; Raeder, Platons Philosophische Entwicklung p. 130; Gauss, Handkommentar zu den Dialogen Platos pp. 139-40.

5. Rabinowitz in Phronesis 1958 p. 115.

6. Rabinowitz pp. 117-19.

7. Although Heidel (TAPA p. 171ff., Plato's Euthyphro p. 83) too

uses later dialogues—Gorgias, Republic, Cratylus, Theaetetus—for supplying the "Socratic" view of the gods' ergon, at least he supports his attribution of hyperetike to Socrates by referring to Apol. 30A. This passage—"For know that the god commands me to do this, and I think no greater good can come to the city than my service to the god" (ten emen to theo hyperesian)—is, of course, very much to the point. Nevertheless for reasons already mentioned I would hesitate to take such statements in the Apology literally. Not only is the Apology, ostensibly reproducing Socrates' speech in court, written in a language appropriate to court-usage, i.e. the language of popular morality rather than philosophy, but a careful reading of the Apology itself in its entirety shows this passage and all of Socrates' references to the god of Delphi and his commands to be deeply ironical. Certainly the kind of hyperesia Socrates claims to have been engaged in all his life—autonomous philosophical inquiry, used here even to establish what the god might mean by making such on the surface untrue statements—is very far removed from, in fact the opposite of, hyperesia as a slavish and ignorant service to the gods. To take Socrates' profession of ignorance, and his interpretation of the oracle "that human wisdom is of little or no value" (23A) literally would be to turn the kind of hyperesia he claims to have engaged in—philosophic inquiry—into a futile, self-contradictory enterprise. (See above, Philosophical Presuppositions).

8. The early dialogues, with the exception of some Apology passages which cannot be taken literally, say very little on the matter, and the later ones, variously attributing to Socrates beliefs which are incoherent with each other—such as agnosticism (Cratylus 400D) and a belief in the existence and perfection of gods (Rep. 381, Symp. 202)—must be used with extreme care.

9. Although in this argument I used passages from later dialogues to show the difficulties of maintaining the concept of hyperetike as interpreted by the help of such late dialogues that the interpreters use in support of their interpretations, the point I just made concerning the gods' incapability of action can be argued, as we shall see later (pp. 120-121), on the basis of dialogues, e.g. the Lysis, which belong in the same period as the Euthyphro and can thus be safely used to interpret it.

14B-15A	Euthyphro:	I will say simply that if one knows how to say and do what is gratifying to the gods in prayer and sacrifice, that is what is holy, and this is what saves both family and state; and the opposite of what is gratifying is impious, and subversive and destructive to all.
	Socrates:	Had you wished, Euthyphro, you could have told me much more briefly what the main work of the gods is that I asked about. But evidently you are not eager to instruct me. For just now when you were right on the brink you turned away. Had you but answered I would have learned from you all there is to learn about holiness. But, seeing that the questioner must follow the questioned wherever he leads, what is it that you now declare the holy, and holiness, to be? Is it a kind of science of sacrifice and prayer?
	Eu:	Yes.
	So:	And sacrifice is giving gifts to the gods while prayer is asking them for something.
	Eu:	Quite so, Socrates.
	So:	So according to this definition holiness is the science of asking from and giving to the gods.
	Eu:	You have understood me well, Socrates.
	So:	That is because I am eager for your wisdom, my friend, and I am mindful of it so that nothing you say shall fall on fallow ground. But tell me, what is this service to the gods; you say it is asking from and giving to them?
	Eu:	Yes.
	So:	And is not the right way of asking to ask them for what we need from them?
	Eu:	What else?
	So:	And the right way of giving would then be to give them in return what they happen to need from us? For it would not be a very scientific gift-giving to give anyone what he has

113

	no need for?
Eu:	That is right, Socrates.
So:	Then holiness is a kind of science of commerical exchange (emporike) between men and gods?
Eu:	Yes, commercial exchange, if that is what you want to call it.
So:	I do not, unless it happens to be true. But tell me, what benefit do the gods derive from the gifts they receive from us? For what they give us we all know, since all the goods we possess are their gift. But how does what they receive from us benefit them? Or is the balance of profit so much in our favor in this exchange that we get all that is good from them but they nothing from us?
Eu:	But do you believe, Socrates, that the gods are benefited by what they receive from us?

In his penultimate attempt to define piety Euthyphro reaffirms two points that have played a fundamental role as background to the dialogue's whole discussion: That piety involves knowledge (ean tis epistetai 14B), is a kind of science (episteme 14C,D) required for doing rightly (orthos 14D,E) and expertly (technikon 14E) whatever activity this particular science governs; and that piety is a virtue whose exercise brings all-important benefits to the practitioner: piety saves (sozei 14B), keeps safe and alive, healthy and prosperous, preserves and maintains both individual families and states, while impiety overthrows and destroys whatever happens to lack this science that would preserve its health and guarantee its welfare. Since these two claims are the basic presupposition of Euthyphro's and the city's actions they can hardly be abandoned at this point, and Euthyphro's reaffirmation of them merely touches on the bases from which all movement in the dialogue proceeds.

What is, at least verbally, new in the definition now proposed is that piety is characterized as the science of giving the gods, in word and deed, what is kecharismenos, agreeable, pleasing, acceptable to them; it is the art of gratifying, favoring, obliging and humoring the gods by prayer and sacrifice--presumably as a means of inducing them to give us what we ask from them.

If piety is the art of this sort of giving and asking (sacrifice and prayer), then, as Socrates points out, he who is a

practitioner of the art must know what is right and rational to
give and to ask for. The only thing worth asking from the gods
is clearly what we need from them, and, by the same token, the
only thing worth offering to them is what they happen to need
from us. The kind of commercial transaction that piety has now
become must be based on the principle of mutual benefit. To be
even immediately plausible and agreeable to both parties the
transaction must provide each what it considers beneficial for
itself; to be practical in the long run, each must receive in the
exchange what it truly needs for its own essential functioning.
Unlike the persons related to each other in hyperetike—an inferior utterly subordinated to a superior's quasi-tyrannical rule—
the parties involved here, however unequal their powers and capa-
bilities as such may be, are equal at least in regard to the
amount of gain each receives. And for the right and in the long
run successful practice of the art of piety a knowledge of the
essential needs of both parties on the part of both parties is
the first and foremost prerequisite.

This conception of piety as emporike, doing business with the
gods for the mutual benefit of both gods and men, has aroused
much righteous indignation and pious horror in some modern interpreters who regard it an utter debasement of the very notion of
holiness[1] and a "malicious characterization" which Socrates em-
ploys for its "gruesome shock-effect"[2] but could not possibly take
seriously.

Such reactions seem to me totally anachronistic. However expressive they may be of modern religious sensibilities, they must
not be imported into the Greek context; they cannot even be as-
cribed to Socrates himself, let alone to his orthodox contemporaries. For on this point—the essential features presupposed for
successfully conducting any transactions with the gods, should
such transactions be ever possible—there is no significant difference between Euthyphro's, or the city's, traditional concep-
tions and Socrates' own. Socrates' objection is not that
Euthyphro's definition is in itself sacrilegious, but that Euthyphro does not know, and, perhaps, cannot conceivably know what he
ought to know in order to practice the art which he defines piety
to be.

From the very beginning, at least from where we begin to know
anything about Greek religion, human transactions with the gods
have been conducted by the Greeks strictly on a do ut des basis.
"If I have ever done such and such for you...remember now and do
such and such in return" was a traditional formula for prayer in
the Iliad, and the situation has not changed significantly by the
end of the fifth century.[3] Those who still turn to the gods in
prayer and sacrifice fully expect to receive benefits in turn for
benefits—honor, recognition, service—rendered. The gods'

superior ability to grant men what they want is the very reason
for approaching them by way of prayer and sacrifice. Indeed it
might be said to be the very reason for having and honoring
gods—powerful protectors and rulers—in the first place.

If piety is to be a virtue—something that improves human
life—it must pay; if prayer and sacrifice are to be any part of
piety, as they were traditionally, they must pay. If they do not
then none of these things belong to, since they do not promote,
human excellence and well-being, and if they do not it would be
irrational to practice them as if they did, i.e. as if they were
a part of virtue.

Certainly no man as a teleological, practically rational being could have any reason for doing something he regards in no way
beneficial for himself, and by the same token no god could rationally behave otherwise. Though the mythological gods were not
exactly prototypes of wisdom, even the least enlightened of them
was regarded to be rational enough to pursue nothing but what he
considered contributory to the enhancement of his own essential
nature and power. Had the gods been deemed utterly irrational no
man could have had any idea of how to conduct himself in relation
to them, and piety as one's relation to the gods themselves could
not have been thought to be a virtue practiced with foresight on
the basis of any insight into the nature of divinity.

The Socratic attack on Euthyphro's definition is not designed
to demonstrate that the traditional conception of piety as this
type of skilled business transaction is eo ipso irreligious, but
that this conception cannot guarantee virtuous—saving rather than
destructive—behavior without the knowledge requisite for its
correct translation into concrete action. And this is the knowledge which once again Euthyphro does not seem to possess.

Socrates is perfectly willing to grant that men may receive
a great many benefits, indeed all that is good for them, from the
gods. (Whether he himself shares the belief, or accepts it here
merely dialectically as a hypothesis whose implications he might
think worthwhile to explore, we shall see later. At this point
the phrase panti delon, "clear to everyone", ought to serve as a
warning. What "everyone knows" seldom turns out to be true in a
Socratic dialogue). But even with our knowledge of possible
divine benefits to us granted, half of the knowledge necessary for
conducting the transaction described is still lacking unless we
can also specify what benefits the gods in their turn derive from
our relationship to them.

But Euthyphro still lacks this knowledge and he still balks
at admitting that the gods can be benefited by us and derive any
real advantage from our doing our part of the bargain—praying and

sacrificing. And this refusal once again makes nonsense of his definition. If one of the parties can receive no conceivable benefit from a type of transaction, the other party cannot hope to conduct such transaction with it as the definition specifies.

The definition fails for the same reason that all definitions in Part II have failed. Therapy implied benefit to the subject cared for, and thus had to be rejected. Service too implied benefit—rendered by helpful cooperation with the gods in their own labors. And both therapy and hyperetike would have required a knowledge of the essential nature and function of the gods which Euthyphro did not have. But successful emporike is to this extent just like successful therapeia or hyperetike: it too requires knowledge, in fact the same knowledge as required for the proper conduct of the previous relationships. To deal with the gods commercially we would have to know something about the essential needs of the gods, i.e. what the gods need (from us) for fulfilling their own function. Thus we would first of all have to know the essential nature, function or work of the gods which was precisely what Euthyphro did not, and if the gods were perfect could not, know. For all its apparent movement all the discussion in Part II of the dialogue has revolved around the same fundamental point. Euthyphro has been running strenuously without moving from the place where Part II began.

This is now brought home with a vengeance in Socrates' comment on Euthyphro's last attempt to make good his claim of understanding piety.

Notes

1. Friedlaender, Plato p. 89.

2. Gigon, "Platons Euthyphron" p. 35.

3. A fragment from Pericles' Samian Oration just about equates the meaning and function of divinity with such exchange between men and gods, and uses it as a proof of the gods' immortality (tais timais has echousi kai tois agathois ha parechousi athanatous einai tekmairometha. Plutarch, Pericles 8,9; Fr. Gr. Hist. 107F9). However enlightened Pericles may have been in his private beliefs, it is unthinkable that would have spoken in terms offensive to Athenian religious sensibility in a public speech delivered on such a solemn occasion.

15B-C   Socrates: Well then, what would be the gifts, Euthyphro, that we give to the gods?

Euthyphro: What else but honor and gifts of honor and, as I have already said, gratification?

So: So then holiness is gratifying to the gods, Euthyphro, but not beneficial or dear to them?

Eu: I should say it is dear above all things.

So: So once again, it seems, what is holy is what is dear to the gods.

Eu: Quite so.

So: But if you say this does it surprise you that your statements seem not to stay fixed but move about, and do you still accuse me of being the Daedalus who makes them move when in fact you are more skillful than Daedalus himself in making them go around in a circle? Or do you not see that our definition has come around, back to where we started from? For surely you remember that a little while ago we found what is holy not to be the same as what is god-loved (theophiles) but something different? Or do you not remember?

Eu: I do.

So: But do you not see that now you are saying that what is dear to the gods (theois philon) is holy? And is not this the same as what is god-loved?

Eu: Yes it is.

So: Then either our previous agreement was wrong, or if it was right then our present position is wrong.

Eu: So it seems.

Euthyphro's final explanation of what the gods might gain from engaging in transactions with men is "honor, gifts of honor, and gratification"; a view as traditional and orthodox as were all his previous definitions and views. The Homeric gods, just like

119

their human counterparts, the mighty rulers of men, wanted, and insisted on being given, the time, geras and charis due to them on account and as a visible manifestation of their power over others. Whether or not these things were explicitly acknowledged to "benefit" the gods, they were certainly regarded to be exceedingly dear to them.

Unfortunately, as Socrates hastens to point out, what is dear to the gods (philon theois) is exactly the same as what is godloved (theophiles), and it is precisely this definition that was found to be untenable at the conclusion of Part I. Thus Part II has come back full circle to a definition already rejected before the discussion of Part II ever began. As an attempt to accomplish what Part I failed to do—i.e. provide a definition that at least delineates the proper domain of holiness within the larger domain of justice—Part II proved to be a complete failure.

Nevertheless the discussion of piety in the second part of the dialogue has been very far from fruitless. For while at the end of Part I the definition of what is holy as what is dear to or loved by the gods was rejected because by itself it failed to define in a paradigmatic and practically useful manner what is and what is not holy, this conclusion still left open the possibility that whatever is dear to the gods does in fact happen to be holy. Even if a man who 'knew' nothing but this about piety would not in fact be able to distinguish between pious and impious acts, his belief in the coincidence of what is holy and what is loved by the gods might not be altogether mistaken. But the implications of the arguments in Part II are no longer compatible with such belief, and thus traditional religion receives a further, possibly final, blow.

To see this we have to detour slightly by way of a brief examination of the Socratic conception of love as presented in the Lysis—a companion dialogue very close in time and spirit to the Euthyphro itself—and later elaborated in the Symposium and the Republic. The combined weight of the Socratic-Platonic arguments concerning the nature of love overturns all traditional belief in the gods loving, and even being capable of loving, anything whatever.[1]

In Lysis 221D-222A love is said to originate in deficiency (endeia) and to be directed toward whatever would alleviate the deficiency which gives rise to it. The true object of love is what by nature belongs to (qua physei oikeion) but is not yet actually possessed by the lover. Thus only what is imperfect—does not yet have, or is not, what it by nature ought to have and be—can love.

Lysis 217A-218C makes the same point. Whatever is perfectly

good, is and has what it ought to be and have, cannot love. Only the presence of some evil or deficiency, and one's consciousness of it, makes one love what one is conscious of lacking and therefore considers good. The perfectly wise, e.g., do not lack and therefore do not love wisdom. Nor do those who are totally ignorant of their own ignorance. Only people in between perfect goodness and badness (in respect of wisdom, in this case) can love.

214E-215B it is pointed out that whoever is really good, rather than being neither wholly good nor wholly evil, in anything, is self-sufficient in that respect, and by virtue of this self-sufficiency needs and loves nothing (in the area of its self-sufficiency).

210C-D connects love with benefit. Only what one considers beneficial, useful, good, will one love, for only such things or persons have a bearing on one's deficiency or evil state whose presence, together with the lover's awareness of it, is the sole cause of love.

The same conception of love is presented in the Symposium. 200B-E identifies one's consciousness of incompleteness as the cause of love, and the object of love as that which one does not yet have, or is not, but is conscious of lacking. The notion of metaxy (in-betweenness) introduced in Lysis 217A-218C returns in Symp. 202B-D where it is emphasized that the gods being perfect—not being in between goodness and badness, and merely on the road toward true excellence, like men—cannot be lovers. Since they already are all they can be and possess all they can possess, they are wholly eudaimones, i.e. in every respect what they can and ought to be by nature, and are therefore devoid of love. Since "no one who does not consider himself deficient desires what he does not think he needs", desire, love, and the concomitant pursuit of whatever one desires or loves are not divine traits. No god, e.g. "loves wisdom (philosophei) or desires to become wise, since he already is" (203E-204A) as wise as possible. Only the deficient can be erotic even in matters of knowledge (provided, of course, that they are not so deficient as to be unaware of their own deficiency), and the same is true of all other objects and areas of love.

In Republic 334C too, loving and considering something or someone good, useful, beneficial to one, are inseparably conjoined, and "whatever one considers useful one loves, what one deems good for nothing and harmful one hates". The proper object of love is what is truly rather than seemingly good, useful, beneficial, and the right conduct of one's loves and hates depends upon one's knowledge of what is truly good and evil.

We have already referred to the Meno's principle, according to which all teleological beings—beings whose telos is still outstanding but who have enough intelligence (logos) to be aware of what they lack—by nature desire, love and strive for what they consider their outstanding telos, end or good. This awareness and striving is in fact the very essence of practical rationality.

There is little point in adducing further evidence. The necessary implication of Plato's just about completely uniform conception of love in the early and middle dialogues is that love is absolutely irreconcilable with perfection, and therefore the gods qua perfect cannot conceivably love anything whatever. Not being characterized by (natural, essential) need, lack, incompleteness and in-betweenness, they cannot regard anything as needed, beneficial, satisfying or good for them, and thus can desire, want, love, pursue, nothing whatever.

Therefore if we accept Euthyphro's strictures concerning the essential perfection and unimprovability of the gods, we must regard the very notion of something being conceivably theophiles (god-loved) to be self-contradictory. The two components of the term, theos and philia, are mutually exclusive of each other. As we have shown, the very notion of essential activity, work or function to be irreconcilable with the gods' presumed perfection,[2] so now the notion of divine love turns out to be equally incoherent with it. This is hardly surprising seeing that rational activity—the pursuit of what is considered good, useful, beneficial, fulfilling—is rooted in rational love—the consciousness and therefore pursuit of something considered good, useful, etc. If love is the very principle of intentional, purposive, teleological action, then loving and acting are inseparably connected, and whoever is incapable of the first is incapable of the second.

In view of this we have to reject all beliefs, provisorically accepted and dialectically entertained by Socrates in the course of the discussion, concerning the gods' relationship to human good and human virtue. For if the gods are indeed perfect they cannot care for and want to do anything. They cannot be the givers of whatever is good for men, simply because they cannot be the givers of anything at all; giving is an action and the gods cannot rationally act or even want to act. Nor can they care for human improvement, the excellence of men, or the "realization of the Good in the world", since they can care for nothing whatever.

Thus even Euthyphro's earlier assertion, left uncontested by Socrates in the dialogue, that all the gods love justice and hate injustice whosoever may commit it must in the end be rejected. The gods, if perfect, must be totally indifferent to all human being and doing since they are by nature indifferent to anything

and everything in and out of the world. Interest in, care for,
pursuit and avoidance, love and hate of anything is simply not
in their nature. (Even if the gods were not absolutely perfect
and unimprovable, but only unimprovable by men, as Euthyphro seems
to believe, the results would be much the same as far as the gods'
relation to men is concerned. The gods still could not conceivably care about anything men might be or do).

Whether or not Socrates, or even Plato himself, really considered the gods perfect, and believed in the existence of such
beings, is to some extent beside the point. Socrates, who in the
Euthyphro expresses his deep-seated disbelief in the traditional
stories about the gods, always focusses his inquiry on human nature and life rather than on divine existence and its characteristic traits. His use of arguments concerning the gods is largely dialectical: designed to show the incoherence of his interlocutors' diverse statements about divinity and to reveal what
human nature is like, as distinguished from what divine nature
is traditionally conceived to be. If any later Platonic statement concerning Socrates' attitude toward divine matters can be
relied upon, the most likely candidate is the Cratylus' statement
of agnosticism: "there is one principle which as men of sense we
must acknowledge: that of the gods we know nothing, either of
their natures or of the names they give themselves" (400D). Although in the Apology Socrates does make positive assertions about
the gods—e.g. that they do not neglect the good man—and claims
to be following the god's command, in view of the incoherence of
such assertions with much of what is established in the Lysis and
the Euthyphro, and the appropriately unphilosophical language in
which Socrates addresses his unphilosophical audience in court,
such statements cannot be used without supporting evidence from
the other early dialogues as evidence of Socrates' own beliefs.

And the situation is not very different when it comes to
dealing with Plato's beliefs concerning the gods. What he says
about divine nature in the Republic passage we had occasion to
refer to is said in the context of providing guidelines for
poetry, and poetry, even under the guidance of philosophy, is
useful only for the education of those who by virtue of their
ignorance cannot yet or cannot ever profit from true, i.e.
philosophical, education. Thus what Plato asserts here about the
perfection and beneficence of the gods need not at all be his
opinion; he may be dealing in a kind of apate dikaia, telling a
likely story which, though unprovable and literally untrue, even
self-contradictory in a strict sense, is nevertheless useful and
indeed necessary for the guidance of the philosophically unen-
dowed. No secure conclusion as to Plato's own convictions can
be based on his engaging in this type of story telling. (The
Symposium's statements concerning the gods' perfection are, of
course, as dialectical as those in the Euthyphro. And they have

the same purpose: to focus the inquiry on man who, as distinguished from the gods, is capable of love, the subject the Symposium is concerned with).

In general, taking Plato's various statements about the gods at face value, i.e. as an expression of his own beliefs, creates immense difficulties. On the whole such statements do more to illustrate the impossibility of saying anything plausible about the gods than they reveal any type of rationally justified or justifiable conviction. If e.g. the gods, being perfect, have no function and work (according to the arguments of the Symposium and the Republic taken together), then how could men, who according to the Republic know whatever they know in terms of its function, end or good, ever know anything about the gods? Indeed, given the inseparability of knowability and being in the Republic, how could the gods, lacking all characteristic activity and thus essential nature and function, be conceived to exist at all?

It is not my purpose here to pile paradox on paradox. But showing some of the difficulties involved in anyone trying to put Plato's scattered statements about the gods together without bogging down in a morass of incoherence should serve as a warning against taking Plato's god-talk very seriously, let alone using carefully selected passages out of context as proofs of Plato's or Socrates' real beliefs. The enterprise requires extreme caution, and even a modicum of caution will leave us with nothing positive to say on the subject of Plato's actual religious, i.e. specifically god-related, beliefs.

As for the Euthyphro itself, and in the context of the other related dialogues' discussion of love and the gods, there is but one conclusion that can be drawn: Whether or not perfect gods exist--whatever such "existence" might mean in view of the perfection of the gods--they can in no way enter into human affairs. We can no more seek to improve or serve them in any way than they can improve or seek to improve, or love, or concern themselves with us or anything in any way whatsoever. Thus all notions like therapeia or hyperetike theōn, and even of an emporike between men and gods, indeed all relationships of any sort between gods and man, whatever form such relationships might take and whether they be symmetrical or assymetrical, are self-contradictory.

This does not make holiness, rightly conceived, any less knowable or any less a virtue. It merely makes it a wholly human affair, an affair to be settled among men and by men, on the basis of their knowledge of what is ultimately good for them. Like all other virtues, in fact as equivalent to virtue as such, piety is a matter of wisdom--knowledge of the human good--and thus the product of philosophical reflection on human nature rather than any type of mythological or even purportedly rational theology. And, since holiness so conceived is a virtue as well as being a matter of knowledge, Socrates cannot give up the quest for it even though Euthyphro himself, lacking knowledge as well as virtue, is perfectly willing to do so.

Notes

1. For a more elaborate discussion see my "Plato Lysis" Phronesis 20/1975: 185-198; also Socratic Humanism, New Haven 1963, chapter on Eros.

2. See above pp. 109-110.

15C-16A Socrates: Then we must begin at the very beginning and
                      ask again what is holiness. For I am not
                      willing to give up until I find out. And do
                      not scorn me but by all means exert yourself
                      to the utmost and tell me the truth now.
                      For if any man knows it you do, and like
                      Proteus you will not be released until you
                      tell it. For had you had no clear knowledge
                      of what is holy and unholy you could not
                      possibly have undertaken to prosecute your
                      aged father for murder on behalf of a hired
                      man. You would have been too afraid of the
                      gods and ashamed in the sight of men to risk
                      doing wrong. I am sure therefore that you
                      think you know clearly what is and what is
                      not holy; so tell me Euthyphro, most excel-
                      lent of men, and do not hide what you think
                      from me.

        Euthyphro: Some other time, Socrates; I am in a hurry
                      now and it is time for me to go.

        So: What are you doing my friend! You go away
                      shattering the high hopes I had of learning
                      from you what is and what is not holy and of
                      escaping Meletus' indictment by showing him
                      that by grace of Euthyphro I have become wise
                      in matters of divinity and no longer act
                      rashly out of ignorance nor innovate in such
                      matters, but will live a better life hence-
                      forth.

    The last lines of the dialogue not only urge that the inquiry
begin anew from the very beginning, but in fact return to its beginning by reaffirming the basic presuppositions which were, and
still are, what makes the inquiry possible as well as necessary.

    Socrates' final, repeated references to Euthyphro's presumed
knowledge--"you know, if any man does"; "for if you did not know
clearly"; "I am certain that you think you know clearly"--are obviously ironical and would be so almost to the point of cruelty,
were it not for the fact that they point not only backward to the
beginning but also forward to the goal of all renewed and continued inquiry: a knowledge of rather than mere belief about the matter in question.

    At the same time, Socrates' concluding remarks emphasize what
has made the present inquiry necessary and makes it still necessary to continue the questioning until it is successfully com-
pleted: Piety is supposed to be a virtue; therefore its knowledge

will not only preserve Euthyphro from wrongdoing in prosecuting
his father and clear Socrates of Meletus' indictment. Above and
beyond these particular advantages to these particular people such
knowledge will enable any man to "live a better life henceforth".
This being the only rational goal of human life, the knowledge
prerequisite for attaining this goal is clearly essential knowledge, the only truly essential knowledge for any human being.
That is why Socrates, or any rational man, cannot "willingly give
up" the search for it. For it is through ignorance alone that
life is endangered and through knowledge alone, and not by means
of traditional, ignorant yet unreflective faith, that life is
made safe and as excellent as it can be.

REVIEW AND SUMMARY

Since the end of the dialogue referred us back to its beginning, we would do well to return there now and review what the
dialogue in its circular movement actually accomplished. For
ring-compositions of the kind the <u>Euthyphro</u>, and perhaps all lit-
erary works with integrity, represent can be successful only if
in a sense their end is already implicit in the beginning and
therefore their conclusion fully reveals and at the same time re-
solves the problems that were implicit but only imperfectly understood at the beginning.

In the section on Historical Background we found the dramatic
setting of the dialogue--Socrates' personal crisis, his being on
trial for the entire conduct of his life--to be coincident with
its real historical setting--the moral-religious crisis of the
city itself, the city's own historical trial, so to speak. It
was this coincidence that elevated the confrontation between Socrates and Euthyphro, or Socrates and the Athenians in court, beyond the level of anything personal and accidental, indeed far
beyond the level of mere history, and made it a confrontation between two ways of life perennially present in the world: one
guided by mere traditional orthodoxy and the other enlightened by
philosophical reflection.

This larger, perennial conflict that the dialogue takes as
its starting point as well as the problem it seeks to resolve, is,
however, as we can see now, not merely the problem posed; it is
at the same time the resolution offered. For the outcome of the
dialogue is merely a call for the continual keeping alive of the
conflict by way of subjecting any and all traditional belief to
relentless philosophical questioning and criticism. Instead of
offering particular positive conclusions that could be accepted
in the traditional, unreflective manner--and thereby contributing
to rather than alleviating the problem--the dialogue offers it-
self--qua philosophical reflection and dialectic--as the remedy
to the disease it seeks to cure. Thus its very form turns out to
be its content, and its beginning, the task it sets itself, is
also its end and the resolution of the task.[1]

For all this seeming circularity, however, the dialogue is
far from lacking in substantive content and positive results. In
offering, as I tried to show, an implicit definition of the virtue that is its ostensible subject—a definition, incidentally,
or not so incidentally, which only dialectic reflection can make
explicit—it also offers a positive way to resolve any and all
moral problems and controversies. Autonomy of thought rather
than uncritical acceptance of tradition; rational human autonomy
rather than theological, or any kind of conventional, heteronomy
is what the <u>Euthyphro</u> shows to be the only safe and reliable

guide to the conduct of human life.

This solution to the problems raised is brought about by a
series of seemingly unconnected yet in effect closely interrelated and logically connected steps without a real break in the
argument.

The first few pages (2A-5C) establish the basic presuppositions of the inquiry: That piety is knowable, and that piety is
a virtue whose presence, makes the possessor's life excellent in
both senses of the word (doing well and faring well) while its
absence corrupts, i.e. lessens the well-being and well-functioning of whatever lacks it--individual, family or state. It is
because piety is a virtue that a knowledge of what is and what is
not pious is of supreme importance to individual and state alike.
Since virtue alone guarantees, and its absence necessarily undermines, the well-being of individual and state, if piety is a virtue no rational being can conceivably be indifferent to its possession and, consequently, to whether it knows or is ignorant of
what it is that it must possess to fare well.

The next section (5C-E) articulates the presuppositions established by elaborating on what exactly constitutes knowledge,
the type of knowledge that is useful for the safe direction of
practical action and is thus a formal prerequisite for the possession of this, or any other, virtue.

Knowledge, as distinguished from opinion, is not a mere
ability to point to particular instances of what is supposed to
be known; it is always a knowledge of eide, ideai, i.e. universal
marks or characteristics that enable the knower to distinguish
clearly between what does and what does not belong to the kind of
thing in question and thus to identify correctly what is and what
is not characterized by the quality in question in each and every
context where the problem of its determination can arise. In
other words, knowledge must be paradigmatic; it must provide a
standard for making practical decisions wherever such practical
decisions are required by the exigencies of life. It is precisely for this reason that only universal concepts can qualify as
knowledge--something of universal applicability—and thus knowledge must necessarily be formal--an articulation of the form or
universal concept—rather than material and therefore inevitably
less than universal, such as e.g. an enumeration of instances none
of which are always and necessarily instances of what is to be defined.

In the next section (6E-8B) Euthyphro's first definition
(what is holy is what is god-loved) which has the required universality is subjected to criticism by way of showing that it is in-
sufficient for providing a clear-cut distinction between what is

130

and what is not holy. Since the mythological gods whose positive
legislation is supposed here to determine holiness themselves fail
to agree in all their loves and hates, and therefore the same
thing may be at once holy and unholy (because god-loved and god-
hated) at the same time, the definition leads to and cannot eliminate incoherence in thought and action.

While the following definition (what all the gods love and
none hate, 8B-9C) suffers from the defect that even with
Euthyphro's stipulation of the identity of what is god-loved and
what is just it fails to define paradigmatically (since it fails
to define what is just), it is used mainly as a transition to the
last step of the argument in Part I. Euthyphro's stipulation
that all the gods necessarily love what is just--a stipulation
that Part II goes a long way toward refuting--and that therefore
there is indeed something that is holy, i.e. universally god-loved,
raises the problem of the priority in the relation between the
terms (god-loved and holy) which Euthyphro associates in his definition as definiens and definiendum (9C-10C).

Is what is holy god-loved because holy or holy because god-
loved? Since Euthyphro is unwilling (10C-11B) to accept the
second alternative--and as I tried to show cannot possibly accept
it if piety is to be knowable and a virtue--holiness turns out to
be a concept logically separable from and prior to the concept of
what is god-loved, and therefore "being god-loved" is incapable
of defining what is holy for the purposes of paradigmatic knowledge. Unless one already knows what is holy one does not yet
know what is god-loved, while if one knows what is holy the addition of "god-loved" is superfluous either for the purpose of identifying what is holy or for the purpose of motivating pious action.

Although the negative outcome of the concluding argument of
Part I is merely that even if all that is holy should in fact be
god-loved "being god-loved" by itself does not define what is
holy, I tried to show that the rejection of such theological, i.e.
god-centered, definition of piety points dialectically to a human-
istic, man-centered definition of even this supposedly "religious"
virtue. And this conclusion is reinforced by the discussion in
Part II which brings home the fact that even the assumption that
what is pious is necessarily god-loved rests on extremely shaky
grounds, and thus the definition of holiness as what is loved by
the gods not only fails to define paradigmatically but is in fact
incoherent with the notion of divinity Euthyphro holds and is unwilling to relinquish.

Part II approaches the problem of piety by raising the question how justice and holiness, two virtues repeatedly associated
in the dialogue as well as in the Greek tradition, are related to
each other. While on the surface this question constitutes a new

131

departure, one not obviously connected with the previous argument, in view of what I consider the positive outcome of Part I the question is in fact closely connected with and logically arises from the previous argument. For if piety or holiness, in the sense in which it is necessarily a virtue, is indistinguishable from human excellence as such, and thus holiness has no special domain of application apart from, and is not identifiable as a mere part of, virtue as an indivisible whole, then the discussion of the relation between holiness and at least one other virtue must show this and thereby reinforce the conclusion implicit at the end of Part I. This is exactly what happens in Euthyphro Part II.

Every one of Euthyphro's attempts to separate piety from the rest of justice by means of identifying it as some kind of relationship of men to the gods fails because on his view of the gods Euthyphro is incapable of describing any conceivable relationship between men and gods that could constitute the virtue he seeks to define and enable us to identify it as a virtue with a special domain.

It would be pointless to rehearse here the arguments designed to show that the presumed perfection of the gods is incoherent with all three types of relation which Euthyphro discusses—therapeia, hyperetike and emporike—as well as with Euthyphro's notion, basic to all his definitions, of the gods loving anything whatsoever, thus making Euthyphro's definition self-contradictory rather than just useless. What is important to emphasize in conclusion is that this outcome of Part II directly reinforces the outcome of Part I: that holiness, rightly conceived, is an utterly man-bound virtue.[2] It is something men rather than the gods can have; something men must acquire by their own efforts, unaided by any relationship to the gods; and it is something men acquire by rationally reflecting on their own nature, function and good rather than that of the gods. Holiness is indeed a kind of therapy, though a therapy of men and not of the gods, aimed at human rather than divine improvement. It is also a kind of hyperetike, if hyperetike is interpreted as the submission and subservience of the inferior parts of the human soul to the superior, rational part, in which case this hyperetike of the self to the self rather than to the gods is at the same time true self-service as well as self-mastery.[3] And certainly one's knowledge of what is and what is not truly holy (i.e. good) will inevitably govern all emporike, all proper, i.e. wise, giving and asking, albeit between men rather than between men and gods. What is truly holy also remains what is truly, i.e. rationally, loved, though by men if not by the gods, and only by superior, i.e., wise, men who know what is truly holy—awesome, venerable, good in human life—and therefore necessarily love it. Such men, wherever they exist and to the extent of their holiness, i.e.

132

wisdom, do indeed have something godlike in them, something supremely pure, healing and wholesome, and do in fact live a godlike, i.e. blessed, happy, fulfilled life to the extent that is humanly possible. And, of course, being holy in this manner they are also inevitably just, indeed possess all conceivable virtue, just as tradition always held though without really understanding and being capable of proving what it believed.

For tradition, rightly understood, is never completely wrong; were it that, no rational reflection on it could accomplish much in its attempt to get at the truth. It is only because traditional wisdom contains a great deal of truth that it can be subjected to the dialectic with success, i.e. with the hope of purifying it by eliminating the chaff from the grain, and of strengthening it by coherently connecting its true beliefs into a defensible system of knowledge. Tradition is far from hopeless and beyond saving; it merely needs the right kind of cure, a therapy that it itself is incapable of administering to itself; thus a therapy that must be performed by the opposite of traditional orthodoxy: the autonomous work of critical intelligence engaged in dialectical, philosophical, reflective thought.

Notes

1. If this seems very like Allen's conclusion, the conclusion I argued against in the section on Philosophical Presuppositions, there is one all important difference: Socratic dialectic is very far from being its own goal in my view. It is essentially subordinated to and a means, the sole guaranteed means, for the good life. That alone makes it worth the effort; it is valuable not in itself but as the road to virtue--the knowledge of good and evil--and thus to human excellence in the double sense of doing and faring well. Without this most worthwhile end-product the dialectic itself would remain just about worthless. Lacking an ultimate product it would remain, like Euthyphro's gods, without a proper ergon.

Socratic "therapy" is, indeed, a therapy of language to begin with, or even from beginning to end. But such language therapy is logically and philosophically subordinated to--since it aims at--a therapy of conduct, and that is its sole Socratic justification. Unlike Wittgensteinian therapy, it is a purification of language and thought in the service of a purification of action and life.

2. And it is with this emphasis in mind that we have to understand much of what Socrates says in the Apology. The Apology's language, is as we had occasion to note, rather extraordinary. (As indeed Socrates' actual speech may have been. At least Xenophon remarks on Socrates' uncharacteristic megalegoria--

loftiness of words--and adduces the agreement of all accounts on this point as a proof that Socrates did in fact speak in such uncharacteristic manner at the time of his trial, Xen. Apol. 1, 4-5). In no other dialogue does Socrates employ the amount of god-talk he does here, let alone attempt to justify his action by so frequent references to what god loves, commands, imposes on him as his appointed task. The terms used in the Apology are especially strange in view of the fact that they are precisely the ones found to be so inadequate in the Euthyphro's criticism of traditional religious language and thought:

Apol. 19A "let this be as it may be dear to the god"; 20E Socrates justifies his action by offering Apollo as his witness, 21B an unimpeachable witness who is incapable of lying; 21E, 23B he claims to be going around on the god's errand, 22A following the god's command, 23B aiding and assisting the god, 23C performing a kind of slavish service to the god; 28E philosophy being his god-appointed, god-ordained task, 30A his service to the god (to theo hyperesia), and he himself being 30D, 31A but a gift of the god to the city, 41D who is fully confident that the gods do not neglect the good man and are not unconcerned about his actions, 42A though the final outcome is unclear to all except the god.

The only way to reconcile this kind of talk with the Euthyphro and the other Socratic dialogues is to keep in mind the occasion of its delivery--its being addressed to an unphilosophical crowd in their customary language--and thus interpret it dialectically: Should what tradition teaches be really true, i.e. that the gods do in fact care for justice and do not neglect the affairs of men and are most concerned with human improvement, then of course all of Socrates' activity, directed as it is at the improvement of men, could be regarded a service to the gods, performed at their command, in their aid, etc., and is thus holy rather than unholy even in terms of the orthodox citizens' unreflective and unclearly articulated notions.

3. Cf. Republic Bk IV on sophrosune.

EXCURSUS ON SOCRATIC VS. KANTIAN AUTONOMY

Socrates' radical affirmation of the autonomy of rational thought, which goes way beyond a mere demythologizing of religion and followed to its logical conclusion denies the ultimate authority of any type of heteronomous thinking--poetic, political, legal, etc.--in whatever sphere of life it may claim to be the final arbiter of judgment, has been justly compared to the Kantian position concerning the relation of religion to rational morality and, in general, of heteronomous to autonomous practical thought.[1] Nevertheless, while the similarities are striking, the differences between the Socratic and the Kantian theory are equally significant.

Kantian morality is the autonomy of pure reason rather than teleological reason and the commands of pure reason are categorical rather than hypothetical--they are issued without reference to and in disregard of the demands (desires, inclinations, pathological loves) of man's empirical nature. Such a radical autonomy of pure reason is antithetical to the Socratic conception of human nature and rationality. Socrates does not set up reason as a counterconcept to the rest of human nature, and does not enthrone it as a quasi-tyrannical ruler which can and must ignore the demands of whatever is other than itself in order to preserve its own absolute freedom--independence of all empirical determination-- in issuing categorical imperatives. The concrete commands of Socratic morality do not come from pure unaided reason itself and they remain hypothetical: whatever is commanded is commanded on the hypothesis and for the reason that it contributes to the overall satisfaction, i.e. happiness of man. It is human nature as a whole that determines what is good--what is the telos of human activity--rather than reason determining it independently of the rest of human nature. Though assertoric rather than problematic, the particular commands of teleological reason remain ineluctably empirical; precepts or counsels of prudence rather than practical laws in the Kantian sense. Since rational reflection on one's empirical nature alone gives content to the commands of Socratic morality, there can be no a priori apodictic legislation here, and all concrete determination of what is and what is not holy/good in any particular case remains a posteriori, relative and context-bound.

This introduces a kind of heteronomy into Socratic morality that is absent in Kantian thought. Reason is not absolutely autonomous here since it gives laws not of itself alone but with a view to the needs, requirements, ends of man's entire empirical-rational nature. In a way, reason itself, for all its autonomy, performs a kind of hyperetike here: a service to the whole man, aimed at a therapeia of man as a whole, rather than a kind of moral improvement that is unconnected with, since not directed at, the furtherance of human welfare here and now.

Therefore, unlike the Kantian good will, Socratic virtue is not <u>absolutely</u> good, i.e. good in itself regardless of its empirical consequences; it is good, it is virtue, only in view of the consequences—the good, fulfilled, happy life—that it is designed and guaranteed to bring about. Its motivation alone—the desire for happiness that is common to all rational, teleological beings— does not make an act good, since such motivation disjoined from and unenlightened by wisdom—the knowledge of good and evil—is as compatible with vice as it is with virtue. And because of this every man is not necessarily capable of achieving the autonomy that is the essence of Socratic morality. In Kant every man qua merely rational is equal to all others when it comes to true moral legislation. In Socrates, however, since mere rationality—what is common to all human nature—by itself is not sufficient to make a man good but prudential legislation also requires wisdom, moral autonomy presupposes and rests on a knowledge which is not something all men necessarily have or are even capable of acquiring. For such men, the ignorant majority, heteronomy of a kind is unavoidable. Because of, and in proportion to, their ignorance of good and evil they will be necessarily guided by someone else; for good or ill they will remain in a state of <u>hyperetike</u>: subservience and submission to the command of others.

This necessary heteronomy and <u>hyperetike</u> of most men does not make the moral autonomy of the few any less important. On the contrary, since the <u>hyperetike</u> of the many is beneficial to them only if it is a submission (of the ignorant) to the guidance of the <u>wise</u>, the autonomy of the latter alone guarantees that the heteronomy of the former will be salutory rather than harmful to them. This is what makes Socratic criticism so important for the success of traditional, heteronomous morality itself: the Socratic critique of all tradition makes tradition itself safe to follow and thus ensures the well-being of those guided by such— philosophically purified and directed—tradition.

Though in the foregoing respects Socratic autonomy as the autonomy of knowledge rather than of pure reason falls short of Kantian autonomy—of reason independent of empirical inclination, and of all men rather than the wise—in other respects it exceeds it, makes human willing in some ways analogous to the holy will of God, and makes human action independent of divine action in a way in which Kantian morality does not.

For having separated happiness in this life from morality— as the mere condition of happiness rather than the means of achieving it—Kant reduced all moral commands to mere imperatives. They no longer infallibly determine the human will: they are merely objectively necessary (commanded by reason); subjectively (i.e. for a will, such as man's, which is exposed to subjective, empirical, natural conditions which do not always harmonize with the objective ones) they are contingent. Only for a holy will are the objective (rational) laws at the same time subjective (natural) ones, for only such a will is "already of itself necessarily in harmony with the law".[2]

Now Socratic morality, being prudential-teleological, involves no such separation—of morality and happiness, doing what is good and faring well—recognizes no such split in human nature—between the natural and the rational parts of man's constitution—and thus introduces no such conflict between objective and subjective, rational and natural motivation. Since in prudential morality what is commanded is commanded as a means, the sole guaranteed means, to happiness rather than a mere condition of being worthy thereof, moral commands are not mere imperatives here: something reason commands but man does not necessarily will. The objective commands of reason (legislating what is good) are at the same time subjectively necessary, i.e. fully adequate to determining the will even of imperfect beings such as men. Since merely to believe something to be good (contributory to one's happiness) is necessarily to do it, to know what is truly good is at once the necessary and sufficient condition of (perfectly) moral action. In this way the wise man's will and action is necessarily holy—in the sense of being necessarily in harmony with the law—and so is his life (at least in the Socratic sense of being as wholesome, hale, well-functioning and fulfilled as it can conceivably be).

This harmony in Socratic thought between the two senses of human excellence (doing what is good and being well) which makes human happiness always proportional to human morality not only gives men the strongest conceivable motivation to moral action but it makes morality untheological in a way in which Kant's was not. For having separated morality and happiness, Kant had to postulate the existence of God to bring the two together again in the notion of the highest good. The existence of God as the "ground of the exact coincidence of happiness and morality"[3] was a rationally necessary postulate for Kant. But no such postulate of "rational faith" enters into Socratic morality. Because of the teleological nature of Socratic reason the existence of God or gods not only need not be postulated as a condition of the possibility of the highest good, but such postulates are in fact incoherent with the concept of teleological rationality. Perfection—in the Socratic sense—excludes action, as we have seen, and therefore a perfect being cannot be conceived of as the ground or cause of anything whatsoever in or out of this world. Fortunately, while divinity qua perfect does not and cannot need men, man, for all his imperfection, does not need gods to be able to conceive of the highest good—the fulfillment of his nature, the proportionality of morality and happiness—as possible. What he needs, not merely for the conception but also for the actualization of his highest good, is not rational faith but knowledge, a knowledge of his own nature rather than of the nature of divinity. Prudential-rational-natural morality makes men self-sufficient and totally independent of the gods. Religion, even in the form of a rational postulation of God's existence and a "recognition of all duties as divine commands",[4] is totally alien to and incoherent with Socratic thought as presented in the Euthyphro.[5]

Notes

1. See e.g. McKinnon's insightful "The Euthyphro Dilemma I" pp. 216ff.; also Gomperz, Greek Thinkers II pp. 363ff.

2. Groundwork of the Metaphysic of Morals, Paton tr. New York 1964, p. 81.

3. Critique of Practical Reason, Beck tr. New York 1956, p. 129.

4. Critique p. 134.

5. Although the Kantian notion of perfection is not the Socratic one—perfection in the literal sense in which it excluded all lacking, wanting, willing and therefore acting—and connotes merely the moral perfection of the rational will, it is doubtful if even the Kantian notion of the perfection of divinity—holiness as the necessary harmony of the subjective will of God with the objective law—is consistent with action and thus with the notion of a practical will. For if pure reason is purely formal, i.e. commands only what is conformable to the criterion of universalizability without self-contradiction, it is purely critical: it determines merely whether or not the maxims proposed to it are adequate to its formal criteria and can thus qualify as moral laws. If so, how can it of itself be productive of any content whatever? While in human action this lack of productivity on the part of pure reason creates no problems because the rest of human nature—the appetitive, pathological part—is extremely productive of goals, purposes, and maxims of action which reason can then subject to its own criticism, what could conceivably give content to the divine will which is nothing but (critical) reason itself? Since God has no other than a purely rational nature, will not His will be necessarily purely formal and contentless, i.e. no (practical) will at all?

Although it is beyond the scope of this study to pursue the comparison of Kantian and Socratic morality very far, it is clear that the one objection frequently raised in criticism of Kant, namely that pure reason with its purely rational criteria is incapable of having any practical causality because these criteria

in fact fail to rule out any action, cannot be raised against
Socratic morality. Since all prudential—teleological-hypotheti-
cal—imperatives are commanded not in themselves but with a view
to fulfilling the nature of man as a whole, a reflection of human
nature and action—in general, as teleological, and in particular,
as the subjective and diverse needs, talents, endowments, functions, goals each individual's action is directed toward fulfilling—is presupposed for issuing commands and fully sufficient for
giving commands concrete content and practical causality.

POSTSCRIPT

We can now return to the questions raised in the Preface and see if they can be answered on the basis of the preceding interpretation.

The first set of problems we had to face there grew out of the intimate connection between the Euthyphro's subject and the charges on which the historical Socrates was tried. In view of the special relevance of the concept of piety to Socrates' trial, we asked how it could be explained that the Euthyphro fails to define it, the other dialogues pay little attention to it, and the Republic omits it from its list of virtues? What if anything does the Euthyphro contribute to Socrates' defense, and does this contribution account for the relative neglect, and even the omission, of piety in the other dialogues?

As to the first of these questions, the interpretation offered here sought to establish that a definition of piety is in fact implicit in the Euthyphro. That this definition could not be made explicit by Socrates himself but has to be made explicit by his interlocutor's or reader's own reflection is understandable in view of the special aim—the active acquisition of knowledge rather than the passive acceptance of traditional opinion—of the Socratic method of education. And this method of education is in turn justified as being the only proper method by the conception of virtue—as knowledge of good and evil—and of knowledge—as distinct from uncritically accepted opinion, true or false—that the Euthyphro presents.

Given the definition of holiness implicit in the Euthyphro it is easy to understand that piety as a special virtue could be neglected in and even omitted from later discussions of human excellence. If piety, like all other "special" virtues, is implicitly defined as a knowledge of good and evil, all further discussion of virtue as such and of any particular virtue is at the same time, implicitly, a discussion of piety, which therefore requires no special treatment. Indeed, if piety, unlike the other virtues, has not even a special domain of application, its separate and independent treatment becomes not only unnecessary but even problematic to the point of being impossible to undertake.

The overall conclusion of the preceding interpretation with respect to the historical problems raised in the Preface is that rightly understood the Euthyphro not only contributes something to Plato's defense of Socrates; it provides a complete and self-contained philosophical defense whose divergence from the one given in the Apology can be understood by taking into account the rather different immediate circumstances and purposes that these two dialogues have. The fact that the Euthyphro's defense constitutes an attack on the traditional attitude toward this as well as other virtues, and a criticism of a merely conventional-orthodox approach to the problem of human excellence as such, not only makes the Euthyphro most relevant to Socrates' own trial as well as the trial of Greek popular morality into which Socrates turns his own trial; it also lifts the Euthyphro above its immediate historical context and makes it a work of perennial significance.

This brings us to the second set of questions concerning the relevance of the Euthyphro to solving whatever moral problems we face today. Should the contemporary reader be at all concerned with such seemingly outmoded notions as that of piety or holiness? Is this "virtue" still a necessary component of human excellence in our secular age? To these questions, too, I believe the interpretation offered here provides an answer.

If holiness is not a separate virtue with a special "religious", "god-referential" domain but is, rightly understood, equivalent to virtue as such, then clearly no one can deny without self-contradiction that he is indeed concerned with what is holy and what is unholy—wholesome, saving, good or its opposite in human life—and no one can claim that a reflection on "this" virtue has lost any of its urgency and necessity—or can ever do so as long as rational, teleological beings such as men, sorely deficient yet aware of their deficiency, exist in the world. By the same token, of course, it matters no more today than it mattered in Plato's time whether or not anyone concerns himself with "holiness" as such. Whoever inquires into human excellence—or any seemingly independent aspect of it—necessarily inquires into the meaning of "holiness" too.

But this does not make the type of inquiry Socrates actually conducts in the Euthyphro any less relevant to contemporary philosophy. For whether or not the particular subject of the Euthyphro, the "special" virtue of piety, is addressed by anyone today, the formal and substantial issues Socrates raises in this dialogue are still very much alive and can be no more ignored by us than they could be by Socrates' contemporaries.

Little reflection is needed to show, e.g., that Socrates' criticism of Euthyphro's definition of holiness as what is god-loved loses nothing of its force if it is applied analogously to positive-law definitions, be they ancient or modern, of justice.

A purely positive, conventional-law theory of justice equates "justice" with "the justice of the state", i.e. the laws enacted and still in force, and holds that what makes a law law (and therefore "just") is nothing other than the fact that it has been enacted by the proper, duly constituted legislative authority (whoever or whatever this may be). On such a purely authoritarian conception of law and justice all questions of the sort Socrates asks of Euthyphro—e.g. is what is enacted (in the Euthyphro god-loved) enacted (god-loved) because just (holy) or just (holy) because enacted (god-loved)—must be answered in the sense of the alternative suggested (pp. 73ff) for Euthyphro's adoption: it is not the case that the law is enacted because it is just but rather it is just because it is enacted. Its enactment by itself and without reference to any prior conditions or states of affairs makes the law by definition just. Since here too what is to be defined (justice) is defined by reference to some agents' (the legislators') in itself unexplained action rather than the agents' reason for the action (legislation) itself, the only difference between Euthyphro's alternative definition of what is holy ("what is god-loved because it is god-loved") and the positive-law conception of justice ("what is enacted because it is enacted") is one of reference. In the first case the reference is to the gods', the divine rulers' love, will or command, while in the second to that of their human legislative counterparts.

But this substitution of human for divine imposition—vox populi for vox dei, the consensus of men for the consensus of gods, the people's will for the gods' love, the human legislators' nomizein determining nomos for the divine legislators' hegesthai governing human custom—is merely a change of reference; it does not in any way change the basic problem Euthyphro has confronted, and all the difficulties the adoption of the suggested alternative would create for Euthyphro are created in an analogous manner by the adoption of a pure, positive-law theory of justice too.

In the first place, since here too we lack an independent (of human enactment) definition of justice, a definition without necessary reference to the will and legislative decision of the people (who assume here the position of the gods in the Euthyphro-alternative), the coherence of all human laws ever enacted can no more be taken for granted than the coherence of what the gods ever loved could be taken for granted in the Euthyphro. And the class of things universally recognized as just, i.e. protected rather than forbidden by law in all states at all times, is as likely to be empty as the class of things universally loved by all the gods and hated by none proved to be there.

It is not merely a historical fact that human laws, at different times or places, are often contrary to and irreconcilable with each other—a fact that was as patent to the fifth century Greeks as the divine ordinances' incoherence was patent to Socrates in the Euthyphro—so that what is just in one state at one time may well be unjust in another at the same time or in the same state at another time. This actual, historical incoherence of the laws is merely the outcome of the positive-law conception of justice which allows, without being able to explain or justify, such incoherence.

143

For purely arbitrary commands, be they human or divine, without
any non-arbitrary, natural basis are totally unrestricted: nothing, i.e. no particular content is ever in itself incoherent
with justice defined as "what happens to have been enacted" (or
holiness defined as "what happens to be god-loved"). The conventional definition of laws qua mere unrestricted (human or
divine) enactment is incapable of ruling out anything as logically incapable of being enacted (by men or loved by the gods). As
far as this definition of "justice" (or the parallel definition
of holiness) is concerned absolutely anything goes.

Now such material incoherence—of all laws whenever, wherever and by whomever enacted—is not by itself fatal to the positive law theory. After all, particular laws, even all particular just laws, had to be no more coherent materially with each
other on the Socratic theory than they are here. Even on the Socratic definition of justice what is just at one time or place
may well be unjust at another, and the justice of particular laws
remains context-bound and relative. But this material incoherence
of particular laws is merely a surface feature of Socratic legislation while it is a fundamental feature of laws on the purely
conventional theory.

For given the Socratic definition of justice (independent
of mere enactment) all prima facie material incoherence of particular just laws is overcome, contrary laws are reconciled, and
their seeming contradiction is explained, justified and dissolved
by showing their fundamental conformity with the basic criterion
of justice—"contributory to the possessor's well-being"—which
is logically prior to and independent of all enactment. But positive-law theory has no such criterion governing and guiding all
enactment, and thus can never explain or attempt to justify the
particular laws' material incoherence by showing their (i.e. all
just laws') deep-down conformity with some prior standard independent of all actual legislation.

By far the worst consequence of adopting a purely conventional theory of law is, however, that pure positive-law theory is
not only incapable of justifying the apparent incoherence of all
"just" laws (laws properly enacted at different times and places);
it is equally incapable of justifying any legislation—the enactment of particular laws as well as the act of legislating itself.
For in the absence of criteria other than mere enactment rational
legislation as such becomes impossible. This is the necessary
result of defining justice by reference to legislative agency rather than the function and purpose of legislation.

Since the laws on this theory aim at nothing (e.g. the common good, the excellent life) and have no purpose or function by
definition, no legislative agency can have a reason for preferring

and therefore enacting anything rather than anything else. Lacking all prior and independent (of enactment) determination of what ought to be law (in view of whatever function the laws themselves have and therefore ought to fulfill) legislation is not only totally unguided qua legislation of particular laws; it has become purely arbitrary as such. For without legislation itself having a purpose—e.g. the promotion of the good life—there can be no reason even for legislating, having laws at all rather than not having them. Thus strict positive-law theory is incapable of justifying the very existence of laws themselves.

And this means that legislation itself—the legislation of particular laws as well as legislating as such—has become an act that is, in Plato's terms, impossible to perform rationally. This type of pure legislation (irrespective of a guiding purpose) would constitute a pure unmotivated act, an act without purpose, thus an act incoherent with the very notion of practical rationality and the essential structure of intentional action.

And should it be performed irrationally—for no reason at all and by means of some random decision-making, e.g. flipping coins or rolling dice—it would be just about incoherent even with the positive-law conception of justice. For this conception defines "justice" by reference to a legislative agency, and here no such agency in the strict sense of the word is involed. Since it is not a rational will determining the choice in view of its own felt needs, desires and short or long run purposes that decides here, no human agency i.e. no rational, intentional, teleological agency, is actually involved in, as a causal agent of, legislating decisions.

Paradoxically, the positive-law theory which has seemed to make the legislator absolutely autonomous and free of any constraint whatever in legislating, actually deprives men of all autonomy. For it is not merely <u>rational</u> autonomy that is relinquished here—since the legislators by definition cannot have a reason for legislating in particular or in general—but so is <u>autonomy</u> in the literal sense. For the <u>self</u>, rational and natural, of the human being with all its needs and desires does not even enter into consideration (of what ought to be law since beneficial to the legislator); it is something other (the flip of the coin, roll of the dice, etc.) than the legislator's own being what he is and willing what he wills that decides the issue and determines what in fact will be enacted as law. Pure positive legislation of this sort—should it ever be performed—is therefore purely heteronomous, and the "freedom" it seemingly provides for the legislator is so unrestricted as to become a freedom from the rational and natural self, a freedom of the individual from itself.

It is hardly worthwhile to point out that "justice" on this conception has nothing to do with virtue--for virtue is that by virtue of which one attains self-fulfillment. Even if we do not follow strict positive-law theory to its radical, paradoxical conclusions, it is clear that theoretically unrestricted enactment--enactment not guided by prior goals, let alone by the goal of individual self-fulfillment--cannot guarantee that the laws enacted will be beneficial to anyone. And since what is "just"-- the laws enacted--is not necessarily--since it is not even designed to be--beneficial to anyone, there are no more reasons for obeying or enforcing the law than there were for enacting it in the first place.

Everything pertaining to legislation becomes totally irrational on the pure positive-law theory. All the difficulties inherent in the suggested quasi-Kierkegaardian solution to Euthyphro's problem of defining holiness arise with as great a force when one tries to adhere strictly to the purely positive conception of law. Human legislation becomes as unguided and unpredictable as divine love was on Euthyphro's alternative; justice becomes as unknowable and paradigmatically undefinable as holiness was before; and justice loses all claim to virtue--as holiness did on the alternative suggested by the interpreters for Euthyphro's adoption.

Though such conclusions seem strange in view of the fact that positive-law theory has never lacked adherents who have been, on the face of it, perfectly rational human beings, it is not hard to understand why this is so. The preceding argument hinges entirely on taking positive-law theory in its strictest sense and following it to its radical conclusions, and this is something that positive-law theorists, quite understandably, fail to do. What in fact saves positive-law theory from being obviously nonsensical is precisely this: that its adherents and proponents tacitly and surreptitiously presuppose everything that the opposite theory is based on, and implicitly rely for the plausibility of their arguments on the Socratic assumptions with respect to (holiness and) justice rather than on the Kierkegaardian stance they seemingly adopt.

For legislation as such, i.e. enacting rather than not enacting laws, makes sense only on the presupposition that living even under imperfect human laws is better--since it enables men to cooperate harmoniously for their own good--than living without law, and this presupposition by itself sets limits to and guides all legislation. If the function of law itself is to harmonize human activity and make possible the cooperation that improves the cooperating individuals' lives, then clearly law as such-- right law, the law that fulfills the function laws are designed to fulfill--is defined not merely in terms of enactment but in

146

terms of the purpose of enactment which is prior to and independent of the enactment of the actual laws whose legislation it in fact guides and determines.

And this presupposition, that enacting laws as such is better for men than not enacting them, in its turn rests on a further presupposition: that it is not only possible to know, and therefore define, justice as such, or the function of the laws themselves, without reference to any particular legislative agency, but that it is also possible for some such agency to know, at least to some extent, what is just: both what justice is as such—whatever harmonizes human interaction and thus improves human life by allowing fruitful cooperation among men—and what is just—serves the purposes of justice—in the particular context in which legislation is needed. Thus both knowledge—of what in the long run is likely to enhance one's own self-fulfillment—and basic practical rationality—doing everything as a means to one's own good—are presupposed here as possessed by the legislative agency. And on these presuppositions legislation is rational but it is no longer unrestricted and unguided by a prior insight into ends, purposes and functions—of the law and of the legislators themselves—which preexist and guide all actual legislation. It is not mere enactment but wise enactment—the enactment of laws that come closest to fulfilling their function of improving human life—that makes the laws just.

It is important to emphasize in this connection that the preceding argument—that any rational defense of law must be based on the presuppositions which underlie the Socratic inquiry into holiness and justice—does not by itself lead to any absolutely one-sided conclusions pro or con orthodoxy or unorthodoxy in everyday life; its practical implications are in themselves neither wholly conservative nor radically revolutionary in any domain—legal, political, religious, etc.—of culture; its acceptance does not of itself either strengthen or undermine disjunctively our reliance on tradition, convention and positive law or custom. Though it aims at discrediting a theory—the pure positive-law theory in the form discussed—it can be used to defend a practice—orthodox, traditional, conventional behavior—contrary to the one the Euthyphro—and the extension of its argument into the legal-political domain—directly promotes.

For it is not just the case that even autonomous thought can lead to actual behavior in full conformity with existing custom and convention—since the individual's own critical reflection may lead to their affirmation as indeed holy and just, i.e. wholesome and good, in their particular context—but that the insistence on autonomous thought itself may be mitigated, and in some cases even given up altogether, and heteronomous behavior may be advocated, for some, possibly many, even most, people, in terms of the Socratic argument for autonomy.

147

Whether or not the historical Socrates ever made this explicit, Plato certainly did, and in doing so merely elaborated on what was implicit in Socratic thought. The Republic, e.g., in no way deviates from the Socratic presuppositions and conclusions—that justice is a virtue; that it is knowable; and that it is, ultimately, nothing but wisdom—yet severely curtails the moral-political and legislative autonomy of most people in the ideal state, even to the point of depriving some of all autonomy whatever. Since in terms of the Socratic argument legislation is not a matter of mere, arbitrary enactment but has its own end and function, the power to legislate in the strict sense—in the Thrasymachean sense of being a true practitioner of an art, a practitioner who knows how to fulfill the function imposed on him by the nature and function of the art itself—can no longer be arbitrarily assigned to just anyone. Only those qualified by their nature and upbringing—ultimately by their possession of wisdom—to fulfill the function of legislators—i.e. to pass just laws, laws that fulfill rather than fail to realize the true function of laws—can be safely entrusted with the task. All others, less qualified or altogether unqualified, must to the extent of their lack of qualification be subordinated to the true legislators' rule and behave, for the most part or altogether, in a heteronomous rather than autonomous manner.

And this argument for heteronomy on the part of some, even most, individuals does not stand or fall with the Platonic state where the philosopher-king is assumed to be already in power; it can be formally extended to any existing state by way of showing that in some way and to some extent some agency or institution within the state may be presumed to have the position of the philosopher-king vis a vis the individual members of the state.

On the supposition, e.g., that any society's culture—beliefs, customs, norms, laws, etc.—at any given time embodies the accumulated wisdom of all previous generations and transmits to each of its members the acquired experience of society, even the crystallized result of the historical experience of all mankind, concerning what is good, wholesome and saving in human experience, a very strong argument can be made in defense of orthodoxy and conservative, conventional behavior. Whatever arguments for this assumption one may find persuasive—be they, e.g., Hegelian in form or based on the affirmation that some kind of natural selection is operative in cultural evolution—they necessarily imply that tradition is indeed to a large measure holy—wholesome and saving—and therefore sacred—not to be lightly questioned let alone set aside—and that anyone setting himself against it at whim does so at his own peril as well as that of his society. At the very least the burden of proof—of the rightness, justice, holiness of his autonomous action—lies on the deviating individual here; traditional beliefs are presumed to have already proved themselves by their very survival, i.e. the survival of the culture they enabled to function well enough to survive.

It is far from my intention here to argue for heteronomy, or even to decide what measure of autonomy and heteronomy of thought on the part of each individual might best guarantee the justice and holiness, the overall health and well-functioning, of individual and society. The only point of the preceding reflections has been to establish the relevance of the Socratic inquiry in the Euthyphro to contemporary discussions of subjects—such as law and justice—that seem to go beyond the strict limits of the discussion—of piety—in the Euthyphro itself.

If it is indeed the case, as I tried to show, that a) the type of questions to which Socrates demands an answer from Euthyphro (is what is holy holy because god-loved or god-loved because holy?) can be raised isomorphically in an investigation of law and justice; and b) the same considerations which prevent Euthyphro from adopting one of these alternatives (that what is holy is holy because it is god-loved) also prevent one's adoption of the same alternative with respect to law and justice (the pure positive-law theory in the form discussed above); and that c) any argument for conforming to positive law, and even for advocating such conformity as a general rule, must be based on the Socratic strictures and conclusions concerning holiness and justice (that they are virtues, that they are knowable, and that they are in effect nothing but wisdom); then the relevance of the Euthyphro to contemporary thought about problems seemingly unrelated to that of the dialogue can hardly be denied.

Establishing such relevance in its turn reinforces the Euthyphro's, and indeed the traditional Greek, association of holiness and justice. For if holiness and justice rightly understood—i.e. understood as virtues—are inseparable even in the sense that whatever problems the proper conception of the one involves inevitably recur analogously in any fundamental investigation of the other, then Euthyphro's inability to separate the two, and the Euthyphro's insistence on associating them, are by no means accidental and peripheral; they lie in the nature of the case.

But the analogy of problems and solutions just dealt with is not restricted to the discussion of these two "particular" virtues—holiness and justice; nor are they the only ones associated by Socrates as necessarily related and inseparably interconnected. The Socratic argument concerning the unity of virtue that the preceding interpretation tried to present implies that the analogy can and must be extended to the discussion of all "particular" virtues and, indeed, to all philosophical inquiry into the foundation and justification of moral concepts. This is important to emphasize when dealing with the relevance of the Euthyphro to contemporary thought, because if the preceding interpretation is right then the Euthyphro's answer to the question it raises not only constitutes Socrates' historical and philosophical defense of his own life but at the same time contributes a thesis to and takes a position within what might be called the central philosophical controversy in contemporary metaethics.

This controversy is in fact nothing modern; the issues around which today's predominant metaethical discussions revolve—the dichotomies of fact and value, is and ought, description and prescription—are merely modern versions and only superficially different formulations of the ancient physis-nomos controversy that Socrates tried to resolve in the Euthyphro and its companion dialogues.

Just as those who adopt and try to defend a purely convention based, positive-law theory of justice adopt and try to defend a position that the Euthyphro's argument attacks and to my mind shows to be indefensible, so do those who insist on the utter separation of "is" and "ought", fact and value, description and prescription, automatically place themselves in opposition to the Socrates of the Euthyphro. They too adopt, and logically have to adopt, the Euthyphronean alternative—i.e. define what is "good" in reference to some agent's purely arbitrary love, emotional approval, or decision—and have to answer the central Socratic question the way Euthyphro himself wisely avoids. If "oughts" have nothing to do with "ises", value with facts, and prescriptions with descriptions, then of course it cannot be the case that one ought to do what one ought to do because of some existing state of affairs that can and must be known prior to and independent of the legislation of oughts; nor can values be rooted in facts or prescriptions be based on descriptions. On the contrary, it is the legislation of oughts itself that by itself creates duties, it is human valuation, not based on any insight into facts, that by itself creates values, and moral commands and imperatives are what they are merely because of some otherwise unfounded human or divine prescription and not because of any natural, knowable and describable characteristics that all the things prescribed have prior to and independent of such prescription. What is good on this theory is good because it is so regarded—valued, commanded, prescribed—and not so regarded—valued, commanded, prescribed—because it is good.

The point I am trying to make here is not that Socrates is right and his opponents wrong—though that is what the preceding study sought to show—but merely that the Euthyphro's argument is extremely relevant to the contemporary debate. Simply ignoring it as an archaic opinion out of step with today's sophisticated metaethics is the first step toward becoming precisely the type of unreflective proponent of the orthodox position that Euthyphro, Meletus, and the Athenians themselves represented and Socrates so ably attacked.

Even the practical, ethical rather than metaethical, results of taking the alternative Euthyphronean position in today's fact/value controversy are almost indistinguishable from the type of moral orthodoxy that Socrates combatted in the Euthyphro. For in practice the relegation of values to some kind of non-rational, non-natural basis as the source of their legislation leads not so much to a Kierkegaardian stance of fear and trembling in the face of utter moral uncertainty as to the adoption of the most conventional, publicly approved of rules of behavior. In the absence of rational reflection on one's own and society's nature and function, the moral agent's "intuitions", emotions, likes and dislikes and actual practical attitudes will, as a rule, be informed and determined for the most part by nothing other than existing custom and tradition. Since no one can in fact live for any length of time in the utter openness in which a Kierkegaardian, or modern, suspension of the ethical would leave man, everyday custom provides the content of the unreflective man's imperatives and lends him the certainty he craves, just as it did for the average man in Socrates' own time. If there is a great difference between the actual orthodoxy of most contemporary moral philosophers and that of the Athenian public it is too well hidden to meet the eye.

There is one last objection to the Euthyphro's discussion of holiness that is, perhaps, worth considering here. As the Republic's political theory is often attacked by commentators on the ground that it contradicts everything our own political system is based on and therefore must be rejected by all those who hold liberal-democratic persuasions and are convinced of the rightness of our own institutions, so the Euthyphro's implications for religious and political thought may seem deeply disturbing to some defenders of our political and religious institutions.

For the Euthyphro's theory, and indeed the Greek attitude to religion, is "totalitarian" in the sense that it admits no clear separation between religious and political beliefs and practice, and insists on the organic interrelation and unbreakable connection of all domains—religious, moral, political, etc.—of human culture. It recognizes no purely private religiosity, and acknowledges no individual, deeply held inward convictions to be above and beyond the constraints of legitimate social jurisdiction. While we today insist on the strictest separation of church and state, private and public spheres of belief and action, and jealously guard by the strongest constitutional means available to us the independence of religious belief from state regulation, the Greeks seemed to have held the opposite view. On the face of it the two attitudes toward religion and politics, church and state, seem to be irreconcilable, and therefore whoever advocates and defends our own institutions may feel logically constrained to reject the Socratic, or Greek, theory and practice.

I think all such objections are merely the outcome of an uncritical attitude toward and unreflective acceptance of our own customs and institutions. For on reflection the Greek view and our own practices are by no means incongruous with each other. On the contrary, the separation of church and state we insist on makes sense only if we agree with the Socratic argument concerning the inseparability of religious and political beliefs and action.

This is no paradox. For on the hypothesis that religious belief and practical social-political action fall into two entirely separate domains, the one having nothing to do with the other, the issue of their institutional connection or separation becomes trivial. If religious belief in no way informs and influences public behavior and has no bearing on any individual action that is of valid concern to the state, then it does not matter much whether or not, and in what manner if at all, it is regulated. Even total state-control becomes merely futile and utterly pointless; it does not become any more dangerous socially than no control at all. All constitutional provisions pro or con the state regulation of religious belief become equally senseless and purposeless. Only on the Greek theory that religious, moral and political beliefs and practice are intimately related, inseparably entwined, all domains of culture being organically interdependent, with each having a profound bearing on all others, can one even begin to argue for and attempt to justify our own constitutional provisions.

For if religious beliefs do indeed inevitably inform all individual action that is of concern to the community, then leaving religion free of state regulation provides a most important means of countercontrol and thus a defense against political tyranny. It is not because religious belief is not relevant to the state but precisely because it is extremely relevant that its separation from political control is useful: that way it can set limits to political action thereby safeguarding it from its own excesses—excesses to which it would be prone if it were itself a totalitarian institution governing each and every aspect of the citizens' belief and practice. In other words, it is precisely because the Greek "totalitarian" view of culture is right that it is important to avoid institutional totalitarianism.

After all, even within the strictly "political" domain, this is how we justify the separation of powers. The three branches of the US government are constitutionally divorced from each other because legislative, executive and juridical decisions each have the greatest possible bearing on the same thing: the just—i.e. safe and wholesome, in the Socratic sense "holy"—governance of the state. It is their inseparable interconnectedness rather than the natural separation of their individual domains that justifies and makes sense of their institutional separation. And separating religion, or, for that matter, any other aspect of culture, e.g. literature, art, etc., from totalitarian control and censorship merely carries the same argument one step further.

Nor is this argument for such separation un-Socratic.[1] If anything, the Socratic argument against authoritarian government—i.e. anyone, be it monarch, oligarchs or even the majority of the people, irresistibly determining the reflective individual's belief and action—went a great deal further than our own institutions go in theory, let alone in practice. No one could be more anti-authoritarian, more opposed to the heteronomous determination of belief and practice and more insistent on the rational autonomy of the individual in every domain of thought and action than Socrates was. This is precisely what the Euthyphro is all about. The attitude it expresses and vigorously defends against conventional orthodoxy's attempts to encroach on and dictate without restraint individual thought and action is precisely what led to Socrates' trial and conviction.

The preceding all too hasty remarks are meant to serve only as a warning against taking the Euthyphro, or any Platonic dialogue, at face value and applying its conclusions or implications thoughtlessly and immediately to our own, or any state's, actual situation and concrete circumstances. Such attempts turn out to be inevitably unilluminating, both with respect to the Socratic theory and our own theories and practices.

What makes Socratic or Platonic theories seem so odd, and on the surface so inimical to our own, is simply an uncritical acceptance of our own traditions that is not based on an inquiry into their basis and justification, and an equally uncritical rejection of Socratic/Platonic thought without a painstaking inquiry into its real implications for political theory and practice.

In other words, the difficulties in appraising Socratic/Platonic theory and applying it to contemporary practice are not the result of any essential incongruity of the two. They are merely the result of employing the method of thinking and acting that Socrates criticized in the Euthyphro as well as in the other early and middle dialogues: traditional orthodoxy, the thoughtless

153

acceptance of what is presently transmitted and believed in, and the thoughtless rejection of whatever seems to depart from it. Since this is the attitude that the Euthyphro most vigorously opposes, reading the Euthyphro today remains as therapeutic an exercise as it has ever been since the dialogue was first composed.

Note

1. Or, for that matter, un-Platonic. What we have to keep in mind before rashly criticizing the "totalitarian" institutions of the Platonic state is that, unlike Socrates in the Euthyphro, Plato was not dealing with Athens or any actual--or, perhaps, even practically possible--state in the Republic. He was devising an ideal state, and only to that state can his particular recommendations be applied in a straightforward manner. That is, the totalitarian institutions of the Republic can be justified only on the presupposition that the philosopher-king is already in power; the absolute authority of the ruler is safe only when exercised by the wisest man, the man whose knowledge sets all the limits necessary to his otherwise unrestricted rule. But for any actual state--states not ruled by Plato's philosophers--Plato would never advocate giving the ruler the absolute authority that only the philosopher-king can wield safely. On the contrary, the logical implications of the Platonic theory as far as any actual state is concerned are precisely the same as those of Socrates' in the Euthyphro: steadfast opposition to authoritarian rule in any domain of social existence, be it political, religious, moral, artistic or whatever. (For an elaboration of the argument that the Platonic theory is in fact a better support for democratic institutions in existing states than any of Plato's liberal opponents realize, see my "Plato and His Liberal Opponents" Philosophy /1971: 222-237).

SELECTED BIBLIOGRAPHY

Adkins, A.W.H. Merit and Responsibility Oxford 1960

Allen, R.E. "Irony and Rhetoric in Plato's Apology" Paideia
Special Plato Issue 1976

—————— Plato's Euthyphro and the Early Theory of Forms
New York 1970

Arnim, H. von Platos Jugenddialoge Leipzig-Berlin 1914

Boder, W. Die Sokratische Ironie in den Platonischen
Fruehdialogen Amsterdam 1973

Bolkestein, J.C. Hosios en Eusebes: Bijdrage tot de
Godsdienstige en Zedelijke Terminologie van
de Grieken Amsterdam 1936

Bonitz, H. Platonische Studien Berlin 1866

Brown, J.H. "The Logic of the Euthyphro 10A-11B" Philosophical
Quarterly 14/1964

Derenne, E. Les Procès d'Impiété intentés aux philosophes a
Athène Liège 1930

Dover, K.J. Greek Popular Morality Berkeley 1974

Fahr, W. Theous Nomizein, Zum Problem der Anfaenge des Atheismus
bei den Griechen Spudasmata XXVI Hildesheim 1969

Fox, M. "The Trials of Socrates" Archiv fuer Philosophie
6/1956

Friedlaender, P. Plato New York 1958-69

Gauss, H. Philosophischer Handkommentar zu den Dialogen Platos
Bern 1954

Gigon, O. "Platons Euthyphron" Westoestliche Abhandlungen
Wiesbaden 1964

Gomperz, H. "Die Anklage gegen Sokrates in ihrer Bedeutung fuer
die Sokratesforschung" Neue Jahrbuecher 53/1924

Gomperz, T. Greek Thinkers London 1905

Grote, G. Plato London 1875

Grube, G.M.A. Plato's Thought London 1958

Guardini, R. Der Tod des Sokrates Bern 1945

Gulley, N. The Philosophy of Socrates London 1968

Guthrie, W.K.C. A History of Greek Philosophy V. IV Cambridge
              1975

Hammond, A.L. "Euthyphro, Mill and Mr. Lewis" Journal of
              Philosophy 49/1952

Heidel, W.A. "On Plato's Euthyphro" TAPA 31/1900

------------ Plato's Euthyphro New York 1976 (reprint of 1902
              ed.)

Hildebrandt, K. Platon Berlin 1933

Hoerber, G. "Plato's Euthyphro" Phronesis 3/1958

Leisegang, H. "Platon" in Pauly-Wissowa Realenzyklopaedie 20.2

McKinnon, D.M. "The Euthyphro-Dilemma I" Arist. Soc. Suppl.
              46/1972

Meyer, R.S. Plato's Euthyphro Pretoria 1963

Meynell, H. "The Euthyphro-Dilemma II" Arist. Soc. Suppl.
              46/1972

Murray, G. Five Stages of Greek Religion New York 1925

Nilsson, M.P. Geschichte der Griechischen Religion Hdb. d.
              Altertumswiss. 5,2.1

------------ Greek Popular Religion New York 1940

------------ History of Greek Religion Oxford 1925

Rabinowitz, W.G. "Platonic Piety" Phronesis 3/1958

Rudhardt, J. "La définition du délit d'impiété d'après la
              législation attique" Museum Helveticum 17/1966

Schachermeyr, F. "Religionspolitik und Religiositaet bei
              Perikles" Sitzb. d. Akad. d. Wiss. Wien
              Phil.-Hist. Kl. 258.3/1968

Schleiermacher, F. Platons Werke Berlin 1855

Shory, P. What Plato Said Chicago. 1958

Stark, R. "Platons Dialog Euthyphron" Annal. Univ. Sarav. Phil.
        1952

Vlastos, G. The Philosophy of Socrates Garden City 1971
        (Vlastos, Cohen, Allen papers)

Wilamowitz, U. von Platon Berlin 1920